AUTHORITY IN THE CHURCH

COLUMBA EXPLORATIONS 1

Authority
in the Church

Edited by
Seán Mac Réamoinn

the columba press

First published in 1995 by
the columba press
93 The Rise, Mount Merrion, Blackrock, Co Dublin

Cover by Bill Bolger
Origination by The Columba Press
Printed in Ireland by Genprint Ltd., Dublin

ISBN 1 85607 154 5

Contents

Foreword   *Seán Mac Réamoinn*   7

PART I: THE ROMAN MODEL

Living with Authority   *Mary McAleese*   11

Structures of Authority   *Bill Cosgrave*   26

Mosaic or Monolith?   *Louis McRedmond*   48

PART II: ALTERNATIVE MODELS

Authority in the Church of Ireland   *Catherine McGuinness*   67

Authority in the Methodist Church   *Gillian Kingston*   79

Authority in the Presbyterian Church   *Terence McCaughey*   88

Afterword   93

The Contributors   94

Foreword

Seán Mac Réamoinn

'The issue behind the issues' is how one of our contributors, Bill Cosgrave, describes 'authority', the subject of this, the first in a projected series of 'slim volumes' in which it is hoped to address questions of contemporary concern in Church and society. His phrase is certainly pertinent to the Church in which he is a pastor and theologian, but we would suggest it has a much wider relevance in the discourse of all Christians today, and indeed of society as a whole.

The word 'authority' is itself far from being the most popular in our world, secular as well as religious. It is too often seen as a dimension of power and, as such, hostile to freedom and free expression. In the Roman Catholic Church it has developed a peculiarly negative resonance, and its exercise is commonly seen as a restrictive and even stultifying force. This book is an attempt to consider a more positive and more creative approach.

Christians throughout history have, in the words of another contributor, Terence McCaughey, seen authority as 'not the property of those who exercise it, but rather a gift to be handled with care,' a gift from God to whom alone all authority belongs; a gift to be exercised in his name as a service to his people.

Unfortunately, it has not been, nor is it, always so. When acting as a function not of service but of power, it is obviously open to abuse and, given humanity's limitless capacity for self-deception, what should be a ministry of love may, even among Christians, become a crude tyranny, fuelled by fear. Or, at the very least, it may hinder and inhibit human and spiritual growth and development, those very qualities for which, in its basic sense of nurture, it should be an encouraging and enabling force.

7

This can be seen and experienced in the family, in political society, in the world of work: Professor Mary McAleese writes of life as lived in these areas, when she attempts 'to unscramble some of the elements of the dynamic of the Church/authority debate'. Her overview (*Living with Authority*) is followed by Fr Cosgrave's close-up examination of the *Structures of Authority*; it is here, in the nuts and bolts of authority-in-practice, that we may see the strengths and weaknesses of a complex ecclesial system and its continuing need of reform. At the heart of this system is the office of bishop, and the crucial questions of who and how to appoint are reviewed in some historical and contemporary depth by Louis McRedmond in his contribution, *Mosaic or Monolith?*

Alternatives to Roman Catholic practice are outlined by three distinguished representatives of other Churches. The governance of the Church of Ireland as an independent Church, since its disestablishment in 1870, is described by Judge Catherine McGuinness; Gillian Kingston discusses Methodist teaching and discipline from Wesley to the present day; Rev Terence McCaughey looks at the Calvinist tradition, with special reference to the contemporary Presbyterian Church in Ireland.

It is, we hope, hardly necessary to stress that, in presenting the diversity of opinion expressed by our contributors, our aim is not polemic. Rather would we wish to stimulate a critical awareness of 'the issue behind the issues', and to promote a spirit of renewal, reflecting the old maxim, *in things essential unity, in things debatable liberty, in all things charity.*

PART I

The Roman Model

Living with Authority

Mary McAleese

'Get that bedroom tidied up, this minute.' It's me. It's Saturday morning and my daughters are sitting in their pyjamas in the living room watching breakfast television. They have been up since cockcrow, the only day in the week when this phenomenon occurs, and their bedroom looks as if the entire Allied forces detoured through it on D-Day. My voice is a tone or two terse-ish. Well, yours would be too if this was the nth Saturday in a row that you had endured this rigmarole. These are not bad kids. They just aren't good tidier-uppers. Yet at the sound of my slightly infuriated voice, they jump up, race to the offending bedroom and commence slinging all manner of objects and items of apparel into drawers and cupboards. Some Saturdays I find myself giggling at the very ludicracy of this exercise of maternal authority. What on earth would I do if they said 'Sod off. Do it yourself Get a life:'?

Corporal punishment is banned in our house, grandparents' sniffiness notwithstanding. Capital punishment seems a mite over the top. But it is idle to speculate on the means of enforcement, for so far so good. My authority has never actually been challenged, at least not to my face. It has never been complied with in advance, in the matter of bedroom tidying, but once prompted by an unseemly roar from me, they crack to attention. So why on earth do they jump at my command? I asked them once and was humbled by the reply. 'Because I respect you.' 'Because you do everything for me and the least I can do is give you the tiniest bit of thanks.' God blessed them, as you can tell, with silver tongues and Jesuitical tendencies. They are all of course still pre-teenage. Bigger issues of authority loom a few short years from now. What I sow now I will likely reap!

All this is by way of prologue to a discourse on the subject of authority, a subject with a considerably more domestic and pragmatic relevance than its intellectual and philosophical pretensions might admit. I inhabit many spheres in which authority of one sort or another plays a role.

As a mother, I exercise parental authority, more benignly than the story above might indicate. As a senior executive in a university, I exercise a degree of authority over my area of control, though I in turn am subject to the authority of the Vice-Chancellor and Senate of the University. As a citizen, I am subject to the authority of the state, which in the case of Northern Ireland is not as straightforward a relationship as it might be elsewhere. As a member of the Roman Catholic Church, I am subject, notionally by baptism, in reality by both baptism and on-going choice, to the authority of the Church. In every sphere in which authority is exercised, either by me or over me, there is the assumption or at least the aspiration that it will result in voluntary compliance, but although authority is a recognizable facet of each of these sets of relationships, its shape and scope is also recognisably different in each. What is more, each of these sets of relationships has become much more complex and much more nuanced in this century with its developing jurisprudence on human and individual rights. You will note, for example, that I did not mention authority as an issue in the relationship with my husband. Ours was the generation which baulked at vowing to 'love, honour and obey', beneficiaries of the post Vatican II image of marriage in which partnership was stressed, and not patriarchy.

It is the subject of Church and authority which is the central theme of this book, but it is almost impossible to divorce it from the other sets of authority relationships alongside which it sits. So a series of forays into those other relationships may help to unscramble some of the elements of them which bear heavily on the dynamic of the Church/authority debate.

It is futile to discuss authority without locating it in both its past and its present contexts. Today's evolving debate on authority grew out of a historic and inherited consciousness about who should exercise power and how they should exercise it. What was valid fifty years ago in some sets of authority-based relationships is no longer valid today. Roles which were previously crudely differentiated into the superior and the subordinate have become much less demarcated but, whereas in the past the larger part of the debate focused on the rights of the superior and the modes of enforcing compliance from the subordinate, today's debate has shifted focus to the rights of the subordinate and the constraints on enforcement. Much of what lies at the heart of today's debate on authority clusters around questions about the identity of the individual.

There was in the old, classical superior-subordinate relationship a clarity of identities which was as superficial as it seemed immutable. How a person was perceived and how she perceived herself were not necessarily the same. Today's debate can be seen as the voice of the inner person demanding a sophisticated recognition of her as complex individual and not as simplex cipher. The demand is for a two- way dialogue about authority in place of a one-way, one dimensional, top-down set of givens and commands. This is a dialogue the 'master' may resist entering but only at his peril, for his self-identity is also crucially dependent on the recognition of the subordinate. A Pope without Catholics who recognise his authority may as well go whistle Dixie.

The outcome of the dialogue is, or should be, a new set of relationships in which the master-subordinate role achieves both a new equilibrium and a new legitimacy. A master who resists entering the dialogue, who insists on wielding the old rule book, on reining in the slackening rope, simply postpones the dialogue and risks talking largely to himself when eventually he submits to the inevitability of change.

The Church is currently engaged in just such a debate, with the upper echelons of the pyramidal structure apparently resisting entering the dialogue, the lower echelons stubbornly refusing to quit talking among themselves and to the media, and a growing body of deserters from the upper echelon seeking political asylum within the lower, thus blurring the normally thickly etched lines of demarcation. That the upper echelon in under pressure is evident, nowhere more so than on the vexed question of the role of women in the Church, where three papal pronouncements in this year alone testify to how closed the debate is not. How many of us remember that phrase, delivered somberly in the seventies, 'The debate is closed.' Unfortunately, it has taken the best part of a quarter century, reams of paper filled with imperturbable feminist critique of impenetrable dogmatic theology and vice versa, for the response to filter upwards. Roughly it translates as, 'Sod off, get a life, watch this space!" The demands for dialogue on priestly celibacy have similarly proved to be immune to the wielding of the papal mallet. The more aggressive the attempts from above to silence the debate below, the more perverse those 'below' seem to get. Petitions are more likely to be addressed to the Pope on the subject of women priests or clerical celibacy than addressed to the Mother of Perpetual Succour for help with exams or 'that the aunt may remember us in her will!'

When an institution the size of the Catholic Church finds itself embroiled in a major debate, its global reach which is the envy of other denominations, becomes both its strength and its weakness. Immediately the world is agog. Mass communication delivers the message from one continent to another. Contagion is, if not quite instantaneous, at the very least inevitable. The geographic spread of the debate lends it a feverish quality. Equally, of course, once the debate is fully engaged and as it moves towards a resolution, the scale of global change it can accomplish is quite staggering. Imagine the consequences for women worldwide if the Catholic Church was to make a serious commitment to eradicating sexism. So far, the papal pronouncements are on the one hand encouraging and on the other hand difficult to reconcile, when viewed against the determined opposition to ending the two thousand year old tradition of excluding women from the ministry of priesthood. Taken alone, that issue is not the passionate priority for every woman. Taken in the context of a Church overwhelmed by the cancer of sexism, it is the icon, the symbol which is the litmus test of the actuality of change as opposed to the mere promise of change. In challenging the

Church's stand on this vexed question, proponents of the female ministry have pitted themselves firmly against papal authority. They rest their case on Christ's authority. The Pope does likewise. They can't both be right, Galileo, can they? Someone is going to come out of this as the loser and recent history within the rest of the Christian family of churches, whatever about theology, stacks the odds against the Pope.

When Cardinal Ratzinger pops his head above the parapet and announces grimly that those who do not accept the Church's teaching on women and priesthood are out of communion with the Church, the response from the partisan faithful is to ignore him and continue on regardless. The days of lying down and rolling over dead because a Cardinal in Rome has roared are fading fast. The nature of authority is changing unilaterally, from the bottom up. Like a wave it is gathering momentum and, defying the usual laws of gravity, it is flowing upwards towards a shore where a line of Canutes await. What is profoundly intriguing though is that this Church, caricatured as autocratic, centrist and anti-individualistic, has within its boundaries sufficient intellectual latitude, integrity and sticking power to initiate, sustain, and drive forward such a debate from its outer reaches, the very place where autocracy is accused of suppressing, if not entirely shattering, the voice of dissent. Given today's freedom to walk away, to reject the church without significant adverse consequences, it is extraordinary that so many are entering this energetic debate with so firm a commitment to the Church and its future. Whether that is because of, or in spite of, our education as Catholics is a riddle, but significantly it is occurring at a time when many other authority relationships are also mutating.

Take the role of parental authority or that which is exercised *in loco parentis*. The schools of my childhood were heavily dependent upon a regime of fear induced by the strap or the cane. Not every teacher in my experience used such props but those who used them liberally and those who persistently over-used them were largely protected by a shield of societal tolerance. The fact that little children were regularly beaten at home and in school struck few as seriously odd or problematic, coming as we did from a culture in which it had, not very much earlier, been deemed acceptable for a Master to beat his wife, servants, children and animals in order to reasonably chastise them. That culture was evaporating as I grew up, but the overhang from its strongly male, authoritarian ethos had tentacles which reached well into the latter end of the twentieth century. Today corporal punishment of wives, employees, even dogs has been outlawed. The use of violence in the so-called reasonable chastisement of children is the last to go. It has virtually disappeared from schools and already there is a growing debate about its acceptability in the home. Personally I despise corporal punishment. For me it is a gospel issue. I am a shop-window for Christ where my children are concerned. Would a loving, forgiving God really stand five feet over a terrified child, snarling and wielding a stick, belt, wooden spoon? I don't think so, somehow.

I know the contra-arguments of justification, in particular those rehearsed in the *Catechism of the Catholic Church* where the old adage, 'He who loves his son will not spare the rod,' is depressingly recited alongside the injunction, 'Fathers, do not provoke your children to anger.' The absence of any psychological or intuitive understanding of the provocation to rage induced by violation of one's bodily integrity, particularly where that violation is repeated persistently and without redress, is regrettable in such a recent document. I can still feel the smallness of soul, the totally devastating sense of personal insignificance, as Mother Brendan of the then, it seemed, inaptly-named Mercy Order, face contorted with rage, walloped, ranted, threatened and terrorised in that lather of unself-critical, undoubting certainty that the exercise of authority without might would produce chaos. Where two or more former pupils are gathered, the rawness of wounds is still evident, even decades later.

The implausibility of comprehending the central message of the gospel, the message of love, when those entrusted with its transmission were themselves caught so irredeemably on the hook of authoritarianism rather than authority, lodged deep in the psyche of many of us children. Our fight for faith, our struggle to believe in a loving God, was ironically often subverted by the very agencies whose function it was to transmit the faith and witness to it in a very special way.

Equally there were, thank God, those whose witness empowered us to believe in a God who knew our names from before we were formed and loved us even 'in our leprosy'. While we have come a very long way from those days of faith by diktat, I remain unconvinced that there has yet been a significant debate on the nature of Catholic education, whether in the home or school, and how in the interface between child and parent, child and school, the nature of Christ's authority is to be translated into a practical protocol governing day to day relationships. When were you or I, as Catholic parents, asked what we expected of our Catholic schools? Where is the questionnaire which follows the event, asking for our assessment of the value and authenticity of vision of the school experience? And as for the kids, their judgment remains in the realm of schoolyard anecdote.

Instead of a modern debate using all the modern modes of insight from empirical research, market testing, consumer feedback and the like, we have had imposed on us a vision designated by the Church authorities, designed exclusively within a celibate male paradigm, a rigidly hierarchical structure which is monarchical in tone. It is a Church which has yet to come to terms with Newman's educated laity, with its consumer rights ethos, its burgeoning jurisprudence on individual rights and remedies for their infringement. It is a Church which is currently in a crisis over authority.

I have grown to prefer the Christ of the light touch, the Christ who loves each one so uniquely and so absolutely that he has counted the very hairs on each head, and to be rather impatient with the Christ who has the gospel in his safe and the Code of Canon law on his desk. There is an image of love I once read which gives some sense of what it is that many of the disgruntled laity are saying about the nature of authority and, in a real sense, about the nature of love. Love is like grains of sand. Hold them openly in the palm of your hand and there they will stay. Grip them tightly in your fist and they will trickle through your fingers. The tighter the grip the faster they will fall.

In a sense we are and have been in the grip of an authority structure with its fist tightly closed. What it seems many of us are demanding is the open palm model. What is more, this demand is
not based on some perverse selfishness or egoism, or some (as is
often alleged) hostile bid for power; it is founded on an intrinsic
belief that the true dignity of the person is only acknowledged in
a system which does not enslave or dominate by intellectual,
spiritual or physical force. The promise of an open, less authoritarian Church seemed within reach in the Vatican II climate and
in the indulgent avuncular papacy of John XXIII. Thirty years
later, the promise has evaporated but the demand has grown
more strident.

There has of course been an equal and opposite reaction, as those
who occupy the high ground in terms of power have sought to
sandbag their positions and to increase their control. If ever they
needed proof of the argument that the tighter the grip the more
likely they are to fail, the evidence from around the world is
overwhelming. The rate of rejection of the Church is on a steeply
upward curve. Those who remain are not characterised by qui-
escence. Among them are, of course, those who are determined
to man the barricades, to defend an unchanging Church, but
equally there are those who are determined to stay and live out
the famous challenge of John XXIII – to cultivate a garden, not
guard a museum.

In the world of work, the master and servant relationship, at
least in the Western world, is no longer the straight line from authoritarian control to automatic if grudging compliance. Today
a raft of statutes, directives and contracts of employment cir-
cumscribe the power of the employer and enhance the rights of
the employee. The employer who roars dog's abuse at staff in
order to force compliance is probably working in a non-union
enterprise of which he or she is the sole owner. Such behaviour
is virtually outlawed in major private industry and in the public
sector. Litigious employees and ex-employees have had their
rights to dignity in the workplace vindicated through the courts,
and it is now commonplace for training to be offered to managers
to sensitise them to the need to motivate staff by methods other
than threats and scolds. Anyone who has ever been to one of

these training sessions will verify that they bear more than a passing resemblance to a charismatic prayer meeting. Buzz words and phrases abound, like 'affirmation', 'encouragement', 'our staff are our best asset', 'staff must have ownership of the disciplinary code', etc. Managers have team briefings nowadays which are much more like panel discussions among equals than generals uttering commands to the troops. Staff motivation is a key to success, and there is a widespread acceptance that effective motivation is not induced by wielding power like a terrorist with a machine gun.

The hierarchical structure which characterized much of industrial and commercial working relationships has given way to the culture of the worker director, and to powerful trade unions. The boss is now circumscribed in how he deals with employees. He says 'jump' and the employee can say, 'It's not in the contract. Try to make me and I'll take you to an industrial tribunal.' True, it is a Western phenomenon, but economics are global, and the abuses of workers in other parts of the world are dealt with now on an international stage where spotlights can highlight, and intragovernmental as well as non-governmental agencies can promote the need for, and direction of, change.

Today the person on the receiving end of the authority-based relationship also has a balancing set of rights which limit and define the texture, feel, expression and extent of that authority. Power is no longer a one-way traffic.

In David Thompson's delightful book, *Woodbrook*, which describes life in the one of the last of the big Anglo-Irish ascendancy houses between the two world wars, he explores the fundamental tension between subservience and self-respect. The servants in the old house were now citizens of a new, free state. Their Master's lifestyle was disintegrating before their eyes, a relic from an impossibly bygone era. His ancestors had stolen their ancestors' land. The folk memory of an oppressed people was a strong *leitmotif* in their lives. Yet they needed work, and work was available on the master's terms. He was a decent and humane man, but when they came to work for him they gave him only their hands, never their hearts, and never their souls. Hearts and souls continued to inhabit a world which yearned for their day to come. The failure of even the warmest relationship between the master and his servants to develop much beyond the purely utilitarian is one of the central tragedies in the book. Outward compliance, built on inherited injustice, is an edifice built on shifting sand, doomed to fail.

The story of the Big Houses could just as easily be a metaphor for the Church – with this difference: that in believing Christ to be with his Church through all time, the prognosis for its future is more hopeful, despite much doom-laden prophecy to the contrary.

That tension between conforming to authority and simultaneously having doubts about its legitimacy is a very strong undercurrent in relation to the exercise of political authority in Northern Ireland, particularly among the nationalist population which is, of course, predominantly Catholic. There is an irony in the fact that Northern Catholics are perceived to be more religiously conservative than their Southern counterparts who have had the privilege of living in a decolonised democratic state for over seventy years. The parlous constitutional position of Northern Ireland has been an ongoing phenomenon since its creation, and each generation has had to adapt to the inherent instability which that phenomenon generated, by coming to terms in some way with the *de facto* and/or *de iure* authority of those governing the State. Perhaps the strong authority of the Church was the perfect scaffolding for a people whose social, political and cultural environment was never truly theirs. Catholics were not members of the government, they occupied no positions of power, they were for many years denied the right to vote, they were excluded from jobs, the police and military were drawn virtually exclusively from the Protestant/ Unionist community and saw themselves as defenders of both Protestantism and Unionism, rather than peacekeepers in a heterogeneous democracy.

As someone who stood and watched helplessly while uniformed members of the auxiliary police force, known as the B-Specials, deliberately and systematically burnt down Catholic homes in my parish in 1969, shortly before I was to take up law studies at University, I have experienced great difficulty in resolving the issue of the legitimacy of State authority and the dilemma of compliance. The complexity of the issue was simplified for some by rejecting the legitimacy and resorting to force of arms, and resolved for others like myself by appeal to the gospel and its tough command to love and to forgive. The sceptics might also say that the formidable power of the State did much to quieten protest about its legitimacy. There is some truth in that view.

The State of Northern Ireland probably has more to thank the Catholic Church for than it imagines, for the Church's structure, its discipline, its voice, provided a framework of reference in an almost surreal world where the law was 'their' (i.e. Unionist/Protestant) law, order was 'their' order, the State was 'their' State. Without that frame of reference, many more people would inhabit the world of spiritual freefall where violence appears justifiable in pursuit of justice. Faced with a stark choice, many chose the gospel – though the choice was not always clearly articulated in gospel terms. Some braking mechanism would not allow them to chose violence. Instead, they chose a role not unlike that of the servants in David Thompson's novel, outwardly law-abiding and compliant, inwardly waiting for their day to come. They shared a sense of injustice with those who chose violence, but its expression was differently manifested, sometimes in constitutional politics but more often in a festering silence, which was the subject of considerable scorn from those who had embraced paramilitarism.

Living with these unresolved tensions, and coping with the daily downstream consequences of a hate-infested and violence-infested society, it is little wonder that the debate about church authority was slow to arrive in Northern Ireland. But the case of Fr Brendan Smyth, the priest convicted of a litany of paedophile offences in 1994, brought the issue foursquare onto the agenda for Northern Catholics. An authoritarian Church, ever ready to speak out on matters of faith and morals, always able to reach into the *Catechism* for the ready-reckoner answer, was for once well and truly stumped. The laity waited for the voice of authority to speak. All they heard was the thud of rapidly closing bunker lids. They filled the silence with their own words, and mostly they were questions. Almost overnight, an autocracy became emasculated.

In the battering the Church is taking on protected child abuse, on priestly celibacy, on sexism and insensitivity, those who wish to see the authority structure mature scent the whiff of victory not far off. Not a bishop or priest can be found who is willing to go on national television to debate the issue of the female priesthood. No counselling service for the victims of clerical abuse exists within the Church, though the occasional bishop says nice worthy things about seeking forgiveness from victims and offering them support, too often as a result of a question from a journalist after the most recent trial of a priest for scandalous abuse of children. Hard evidence of practical support is not very forthcoming.

Police, courts, secular agencies and the media have all filled the vacant spaces. They will be hard to shift. The seven-hundred-page *Catechism*, the three-hundred-page *Code of Canon Law* are of little assistance. A bishop speaks off the cuff in favour of a debate on celibacy. The heavens open, deluges fall and he is summoned ominously to Rome. A priest systematically abuses children for four decades, is quickly shifted from parish to parish as each new accusation surfaces. No call to Rome, no deluge – until investigative journalists scrape the surface, and then there is a deluge of a different order entirely. No one in authority appears to be appalled by this curious differential in approach to deviance. Everyone else is catatonic with incredulity!

Under pressure, the holes in this once firm edifice of hierarchical authority are shown up in sharp relief. Like the kissing of bishop's rings and automatic deference, the old ways have mutated under our noses. Consent to the processes of authority, rather than to the authority itself, is intensely problematic. The roar from behind the barricades in Rome is a bluff, and it is being called. Importantly, it is not being called out of spite, nor out of gratuitous mischief-making. It is being called out of an impulse which is Christ-centered and which is determined to shift the gravitational pull of the Church back to an authentic vision of

Christ, and away from narrow clerical institutionalism. It is of course informed by a model of Western democratic authority, in which legitimacy stems from approbation by the subject expressed through the ballot box. Authorities big and small are now held accountable, by reference to the subjects' evaluation of their performance or the evaluation of an agency acting on the subjects' behalf. No such forum exists within the Church, neither ballotbox nor ombudsman. In their absence and in the absence of anything equivalent, the newspaper pages and radio and television greedily, ravenously fill the void. Megaphone diplomacy conducted over the airwaves is no substitute for getting one's house in order.

Where are the examples of the structure we could have and should have? As the *Catechism* says, authority does not derive moral legitimacy from itself. It derives from God. Looking afresh at Luke's gospel, I was stunned by the story of the encounter between Mary and the Angel Gabriel. As the story was taught to me, it was the classic expression of the authority relationship between the individual and God. Mary's words were portrayed as evidence of a humble submission to God's will for her. Those words, 'Be it done unto me according to thy word,' have rung down through the centuries as the template for instant and unquestioning submission from us lesser mortals. But this edited and collapsed version of the story is ingenuous, and misses the point. In the first place, the all-powerful God, who could have dumped Mary right into it without as much as a by your leave, sent an emissary to her to set before her the Master's plan. Gabriel's opening words are a wonderful endorsement of the loving respect in which God holds his people. He salutes her, for 'she is full of grace and blessed among women!' Mary is not, however, seduced by what could pass for flattery. Instantly she is questioning and sceptical. What on earth is this whole thing about? 'She was much perplexed at hearing him speak so, and cast about in her mind, what she was to make of such a greeting.' The angel saw her fear. He could have ignored it, told her to knuckle down to the Lord's will. 'Anyone who doesn't do the Lord's will is out of communion with the Lord,' he could have said. Instead, holding her metaphorically in his open palm, he allayed her fears: 'Mary, do not be afraid,' he says gently, as he sets out God's desired, but not mandated, schedule for her life But still Mary is unconvinced. 'How?' she asks, and 'Why?' It is the angel's next reply which is crucial. Something in it, something in his demeanour, strikes a chord in her. Now she believes that this is truly God's will. Now she decides that she will make God's will her will. It is her decision, freely made, in faith. Would God have huffed if she had said 'no'? Would he have said 'The debate is over'?

Later, when Mary meets Elizabeth, she is radiant with joy, not just because she is to bear the Christ child, but because she has fully comprehended the relationship between God and his people. God has looked graciously upon the lowliness of his handmaid. He is Master, she is servant, but this is an open relationship with a depth of mutual respect so profound it is hard to accept, but a liberating joy to experience He does indeed have mercy on us.

Authority without mercy fails the test of Christ-centredness. The absence of mercy is a fair indicator that authority has become over-concerned with power. Its veins have become clogged up with bureaucratic endeavour, with head counting rather than heart counting. The debate about authority in the Church is a cry for mercy, the authentic mercy of God himself, the self-same mercy offered to Peter, the rock on whom the Church was founded – a coward and a liar, who failed Christ in Gethsemane and failed him again outside the High Priest's palace. The days of the head count are ending. Courting of the heart and mind, patience in the face of dissent and scepticism, openness to the voice of challenge and question, mercy in the teeth of rejection and hurt, humility and reparation in the light of mistakes and injustices, these will be the hallmarks of the authority structure which will serve the Church of the next millennium. As the *Catechism* says, 'The duty of obedience requires all to give due honour to authority and to treat those who are charged to exercise it with respect and, *insofar as it is deserved*, with gratitude and good will.'

But there is another duty which transcends the duty of obedience to authority, and that is the obligation to promote the common good, to participate in the public life of the Church and to contribute to its wellbeing. The *Catechism* recognises that the dignity of the human person needs to be supported by institutions which protect and improve the conditions of human life in all its spheres, whether spiritual or temporal.

The cloak of Christ has never prevented his Church from making grievous errors. It has simply ensured its survival despite them. To those who believe authority is entitled to unquestioning obedience, check the text. Respect and honour do not come automatically with the job. Obsequiousness is a poor imitation of them, though often mistaken or substituted for them. Today they are earned the hard way. As we sow, so shall we reap.

Someday, God willing, my children will have their own houses and the state of their bedrooms will be their own business. Will they have their faith? Will they still be members of this great and exasperating family which is the Catholic Church? I trust in God they will. Trusting in man is not a comforting thought for, while our Church flagellates itself, consuming its vast energy in a debate about itself, the world of mankind is marching on. Technology is outstripping ethics. Total power over life and death on the entire planet rests in the hands of a tiny number of world leaders. We need a strong Church, we need a united and refreshed Church, we need an intellectually and spiritually credible Church. There may, in the future, be other authorities issuing orders with whose consequences no human being should be asked to live. Then we will need men and women who can say 'no', clearly and firmly.

Structures of Authority

The issue behind the issues today

Bill Cosgrave

You would need to be a very unperceptive member or observer of the Roman Catholic Church in our day not to know that all is not well. The many sexual and other scandals and controversies have done much to damage the standing and influence of hierarchy and clergy among the laity, and in society in general. Many, rightly or wrongly, link these disturbingly numerous problems with the issue of obligatory celibacy for diocesan priests, and thus point to what they see as a common root behind the surface problems. Whatever about this link, there is no doubt that celibacy presents a difficulty for many priests today. But it is by no means the only significant problem that the Church is confronted with at the present time. There is a host of issues that show no signs of going away and that concern a great many church members, either directly or indirectly.

These include such contentious matters as the absolute ban on the admission to communion of divorced and remarried people; the ordination of married men; the anomaly of former Anglican clergymen who are married being ordained as Catholic priests, while Catholic priests who have married are excluded totally from priestly ministry; questions in sexual ethics like contraception, homosexual relationships, artificial reproductive techniques and divorce; the issue of women in the Church, and in particular the ordination of women; the appointment by the Vatican of very conservative bishops, often against the wishes of the local Church; the disciplining of progressive theologians by the Vatican, and the concomitant growth of an atmosphere of fear within the theological community; the imposition of a new oath of fidelity on nearly all important office holders in the Church, and the extension of the profession of faith to include all the provisions of the Code of Canon Law and almost all papal teaching; the total rejection by the Vatican of all public dissent from any church teaching; the virtual elimination of all real collegiality in the higher levels of church government; and so on.

And, underlying these, there is another issue or set of issues that has/have a big bearing on whether and how these problems are or are not brought to resolution. This is the matter of authority in the Catholic Church and in particular the structures of that authority, i.e. the way in which power is located, distributed and used. In other words, the root issue or problem that must be addressed, if the Catholic Church is to deal adequately with the specific questions mentioned above, is a structural one. One writer puts it as follows: underlying the obvious issues is a hidden agenda that blocks their solution at every turn. The hidden agenda is not a matter of something that someone is trying to hide or is even aware of hiding. It is simply authority in the Church and our assumptions about it.[1] In a nutshell, this structural problem can be seen as religious monarchy, threatening to overwhelm the beginnings of religious democratisation in the Catholic Church.[2]

This chapter will be devoted to a discussion of this issue and how it impacts on at least some of the specific problems of church teaching, law and policy already referred to.

When it comes to authority and its structures in the Catholic Church we tend to think automatically of the Pope and the Curia, and in particular perhaps of papal infallibility. This is understandable and right, because there resides the highest authority in the Church in regard to both teaching and jurisdiction. However, the issue and our discussion cannot be confined to this papal dimension only. We need to look at the structures of authority at *all* levels, how they are and should be set up, understood and made use of. This will involve us looking at the papacy in its relation to the bishops and local Churches. We will also need to focus on the understanding and exercise of the episcopal ministry at the diocesan level, and how it relates and should relate to the other structures of authority, actual or possible, within the diocese. Finally, we must concern ourselves with the parish, its clergy and laity, and how they interact, and what structures of authority do and should exist at that basic level.

But first, it will be helpful to examine some background matters in terms of history, the theology of Vatican II, and post-conciliar theological and pastoral developments.

Pre-Vatican II position on structures of authority

There is no disputing the fact that for a very long time before Vatican II, and in particular from the time of Vatican I in 1869-70, the dominant understanding or model of the Church, and so of its authority structures, was what is referred to today as the institutional or 'pyramid' model. This viewed the Church from above, as it were; it was a high ecclesiology. At all levels, and especially at the level of the papacy, the judgments of Church authorities were unquestioned and indeed unquestionable. And corresponding to this, the central virtue in Catholic practice at all levels was obedience, indeed even blind obedience. A big factor in consolidating this understanding and practice was the definition by Vatican I of the jurisdictional primacy of the Pope over the whole Church: the Roman Pontiff has full and supreme power of jurisdiction in the universal Church. This power is truly episcopal, ordinary and immediate over each and all Churches and over each and all the faithful. This was further reinforced by the declaration of the Pope's infallibility. As a result of this latter, every act of the Pope became suffused with an aura of authority that went beyond what it had by its nature as papal teaching, and that some have referred to as creeping infallibility. Thus the Church became even more centralised, even more institutional and pyramidal. And this percolated down to the levels of the diocese and the parish, and was reflected in the manner in which bishops and priests in parishes exercised their authority and understood their role.

In this context, collegiality, subsidiarity and similar participative and democratising attitudes and practices were given little place in theory or practice at any level. Practically all decisions, especially important ones, were made from above and handed down with little or no consultation or participation of interested parties, whether these were bishops, priests or lay people. And this was regarded as normal, and no one questioned it. Thus bishops were appointed by the Vatican with little regard for the wishes of the diocese involved. At diocesan level, bishops made appointments to parishes and curacies, not merely without consulting the people the priests were being sent to, but usually without any attention to the wishes or even the talents of the priest being appointed. Within parishes, priests frequently ran a one-man show and what the laity thought or said was largely ignored. They were not infrequently reduced to the roles of paying, praying and obeying, and they accepted that that was the way things were.

Clearly, in such a conception of the Church authority was highly centralised, and totally clerical. The structures favoured authoritarian rule, and the vast majority of those affected were excluded from power and decision-making, and were passive recipients of whatever those at the top decided.

This understanding and operation of the structures of authority makes the exercise of that authority easier and more decisive; there is usually little questioning of the decisions made, and so the whole community marches forward on the one step; life is ordered by clear and definite rules that are rarely disputed; all the members have to do is to inform themselves of the decisions and rules of those in authority and obey them; there is usually little ambiguity and uncertainty and, hence, people tend to feel secure, sure of their identity and role and clear about what is expected of them. As against all this, most people are reduced to a very passive state with no say in the running of the Church community; they are largely excluded from responsibility, decision-making and active participation in church life, whether at episcopal, clerical or lay level; they are rendered exceedingly dependent on authority, and, as a result, their growth to Christian maturity is slowed down or even halted. In addition, scripture scholars and theologians have not been slow to point out that such a model of the Church seems significantly at odds with the New Testament account of Jesus' exercise of authority, and with the structures and exercise of authority in the early Church. In the light of all this, the pyramid model can be seen to

be an historical development and, hence, not necessarily un-
changeable or of divine origin.

It may be added here that Vatican I's strong teaching on the primacy of the Pope was not altogether free from ambiguity and
unhelpful implications. The main one referred (and still refers)
to the relationship between the Pope's power within any particular diocese and that of the local bishop. Some put it starkly, and
wondered was the Pope not now the bishop of every diocese
and was the local bishop not, then, dispensable or at best a mere
agent of the papacy? Despite assurances that this is not so, it is
not fully clear that papal primacy, at least in theory, is fully respectful of the authority of local bishops in their own dioceses.
In the present pontificate, when papal interventions in local
Churches are more frequent than earlier, and often controversial,
this question is especially pressing. Even Vatican II did not re-
solve it, despite its extensive attention to the office of bishop in
the Church and the relationship of the bishop to the Pope.

But, notwithstanding this point, Vatican II changed the Church's
self-understanding in general, and especially in relation to authority and its structures and exercise, in profound and perma-
nent ways.

Vatican II's teaching on authority and its structures

The central point of relevance here is that the Council's
Constitution on the Church (*Lumen Gentium*) moved from seeing
the institutional model of the Church as the dominant one, to
placing the idea of the Church as the People of God at the centre
of its thinking. This has profound implications for authority in
the Church and for its structures. No longer is it possible to
equate the Church with the hierarchy or the papacy, nor to view
it as an absolute monarchy with the Pope as the repository of all
power. Now it is clear that, in the first place, the Church is the
community of disciples of Christ, the People of God, united by
baptism and all having a fundamental dignity and equality as
children of God, and brothers and sisters of Christ. Hence, each
member, just because he/she is a member, has a role to play in
the Church and is called to full, active and conscious participation, both in the eucharist, and in the life of the Church generally.

In addition, this Church is in history, and is still on pilgrimage to its final goal, the kingdom of God in its fullness. Hence, the Church as it exists at any time is imperfect, and, so, it can and should grow, change and develop in important ways, even in its structures, as it has done significantly in the past.

Only when all this has been said, does the Council come to discuss office and hierarchy in the Church. Office is to be understood in terms of service to God's People and not in terms of domination, as had been the case often in the past. In addition, the very significant idea of *collegiality* between the Pope and the bishops of the Church is firmly taught in *Lumen Gentium*, 2. Here was a recovery of a very ancient concept and practice in the Church, by which bishops are linked to one another and to the bishop of Rome by the bonds of unity, charity and peace. This collegial nature of the body of bishops is expressed chiefly in ecumenical councils but in other ways too. It means that all bishops have a corporate responsibility for the unity of faith and of communion in the universal Church. While continuing to affirm the primacy of the Pope in terms of Vatican I, the Council sees the order of bishops as the successor of the 'college' of the apostles. in teaching authority and pastoral rule and, hence, as the subject of supreme and full power over the universal Church.

This teaching on collegiality resulted from a return to the New Testament, and from an openness to the ways authority was structured in the infant Church and the early Christian centuries. But Vatican II only sketched out the broad lines of the principle of collegiality, and didn't detail what its implications and expressions might be. One could assume that it would be rich with consequences, especially in relation to structures of authority involving the bishops. Examples are the synod of bishops, episcopal conferences, diocesan pastoral councils, councils of priests, national conferences of priests, etc..

All that has been said so far about the teaching of Vatican II does not, however, give us the full picture. The other side of the coin is that, understandably, the Council repeated all that Vatican I had taught about the papacy, and in particular about the Pope's primacy of jurisdiction and his infallibility, while also developing Church teaching on the episcopal office.

Vatican I, as we noted earlier, left unresolved the problem of the relationship between the Pope and individual bishops *in their dioceses*. Vatican II did likewise, and may have added to the problem by its fuller theology of the episcopate. In addition to this, Vatican II by its teaching on collegiality raised another problem, namely, how to reconcile the fact that the Pope has supreme, full and universal authority over the Church with the fact that the college of bishops has the same power. Furthermore, the Council discussed collegiality as pertaining largely to the papal-episcopal level, and while open to it at all levels, e.g. bishop and priests, priests and laity, it was not as clear and unequivocal about these other levels as one might have wished. This has given room to more conservative or authoritarian pastors and theologians to maintain their attitudes and the non-participative structures they tend to prefer.

It is also true that, since *Lumen Gentium* is in important ways a compromise document, as between the more conservative and the more progressive bishops at the Council, it is open to being quoted selectively to suit one's preference in relation to Church structures. In consequence some have stressed the collegial, participative, democratising elements, while others re-affirm the Vatican I perspectives that favour more monarchical, authoritarian attitudes and structures. Thus, Vatican II is invoked by both groups in the Church today, conservatives and progressives, in ways that have fuelled post-conciliar debates and controversies, as well as providing for all a basis for unity and enrichment in regard to our understanding of the Church itself.

Post-conciliar developments: ambiguity and conflict

While the Catholic Church in our day is split into a conservative and a progressive wing, there is, of course, a silent majority not aligned with either group's attitudes and activities, and not very aware of them either. But the fact of a real polarisation is indisputable. This division is based ultimately on theological differences, rooted in contrasting ecclesiologies and, in particular, in differing theologies of authority. These differing theologies are *both* grounded in the teaching of Vatican II, with all the ambiguities and differing emphases we have adverted to. Thus, it becomes clear that the issue behind the issues in dispute between conservatives and progressives, is that of authority, and how it should be understood, structured and used.

It seems clear too that, in this conflict, the Pope and the Curia have in the present pontificate aligned themselves with, and indeed led, the conservative tendency who are not slow to assert that their own position is 'the Church's' position. In all this we find a Vatican I perspective that is, of course, to be found in Vatican II, but does not represent the main thrusts of that Council.

The group of theologians, pastors and even bishops who are often referred to as progressives or, more derogatorily today, as liberals, base their thinking, attitudes and judgements on the more characteristic teachings of Vatican II. These are the teachings that emphasise the role and importance of the local Church, that call us to greater respect for and use of the principles of collegiality and subsidiarity, that urge all to full participation in Church life, that put high store on the ancient principle that what touches all as individuals should be approved by all, and so on. In short, the thrust of Vatican II towards democratisation grounds the views of the progressive wing on the Church itself, on its structures of authority and its pastoral decisions and policies. In this stance, it seems that this group is more true to the intention and attitude of Vatican II than the conservative wing, which has in effect sidelined *Lumen Gentium*, or at best pays lip service to its distinctive ecclesiology. In practice, they go a long way towards replacing it by Vatican I's *Pastor Aeternus*, with its monarchical and authoritarian attitudes, tendencies and practices.

Symbolising this conflict: attitudes to dissent

At this point, it may be useful to discuss briefly one issue in Church life today that can function as a kind of symbol of the polarisation referred to. This is the issue of theological and pastoral dissent or disagreement. The contrasting attitudes to it mirror and sum up the contrasting ecclesiological attitudes and practices we have been outlining.

The Vatican, especially through the actions of the Congregation for the Doctrine of the Faith (CDF), headed by Cardinal Ratzinger, has made it abundantly clear in recent years that it sees no place whatever for public dissent from the teachings of the Church's official Magisterium or Teaching Office. The CDF judges that such dissent is wrong and it has issued a variety of documents expressing this view clearly and strongly. In addition, the CDF has laid down and imposed disciplinary measures against those it regards as dissenting theologians and pastors, e.g. Hans Küng, Charles Curran, Leonardo Boff, Archbishop Hunthausen and Bishop Gaillot (France).

Those whom I have been calling the conservative element, and especially some articulate groups and individuals within it, have been and are very vociferous in their support for all this, and indeed they have not been slow to call for Vatican condemnation of any theologians or pastors they judge to be public dissenters. It seems clear that Rome has listened to many of these calls, and has responded positively to them. Hence, the spate of cases where theologians have been removed from their teaching posts and declared no longer Catholic theologians, or have been silenced for a period. Hence, also, the cases where imprimaturs have been withdrawn from books of theology on the Vatican's orders, and where even bishops have been removed from office or have had their ordinary powers curtailed significantly. It is in pursuit of their campaign to crack down on public dissent, that the CDF has, as already noted, imposed a new and more extensive 'profession of faith' on many office holders in the Church, and now also requires an oath of loyalty from a great number of Church personnel as they assume any of a great variety of offices. It does not seem too far fetched to surmise also that the new catechism, which was strongly advocated and called for by many conservative voices at and outside the special Synod of Bishops in 1985, was not written merely to provide 'a sure and authentic reference text for ... preparing local catechisms.' In the minds of at least some of its supporters, and probably in that of the CDF also, the compilation of such a universal catechism had and has a 'political' purpose, namely, to provide a norm or standard by which 'liberal' theologians and writers could be checked and judged and, then, appropriately disciplined.

All these attitudes and measures in relation to dissent today reflect an ecclesiology that breathes a spirit other than that of the main thrusts of *Lumen Gentium* and that seems to understand the relevant structures of authority in an institutional manner. Hence, any questioning of, or inability to accept, Church teaching is rejected as damaging to the unity of the Church and as lacking the requisite loyalty and spirit of submission that all Catholics must have towards the Magisterium and its teaching, even non-infallible teaching. In addition, this view asserts, the faithful have a right not to be confused about Church teaching by discordant and dissenting opinions from theologians and others. In consequence of this view, such dissent is seen as wrong and as something that may well call for disciplinary measures. A common way in which those who dissent from any of the Church's official teachings are today labelled is to speak of them as *à la carte* Catholics, i.e. those who take only what they like and leave the teachings they do not fancy. In this view, the truly loyal Catholic accepts and holds dear *all* the Church's official teachings. Those who dissent on any issue are, then, branded as disloyal. Some who are particularly fond of using a military model to understand the Church – they see the Church as the army of Christ sent to do battle in and against the world and its forces of evil – are not slow to suggest that those who cannot accept all the Church's teachings fully and, hence, are not fully obedient to the leaders of the Church, should simply leave the Church, there being a place in it, as in any army, only for those who can give total obedience.

Those who make up the so called progressive group see things rather differently. Viewing the Church as the pilgrim People of God, they see the search for the fullness of truth as ever ongoing and never complete. The whole Church is learning, and has to learn continually, while in a real sense the whole Church is a teaching Church, as it socialises its new members and deepens the faith and understanding of all who belong to it. As the Church thus learns and teaches, it will inevitably be the case that proposals and suggestions will be made in relation to particular religious and moral issues; some will be good and acceptable, while others will not survive discussion and debate. Occasionally

Church leaders may need to intervene to point out errors and give indications of the best paths to take in the search for truth. Warnings may even be necessary and, at times, the rejection of some moral or theological position. Disciplinary measures may occasionally be taken. But overall, the emphasis of the Church's leadership should be on promoting the search for truth in a positive manner and building an atmosphere of trust and co-operation between theologians, bishops and the Vatican, something like the harmonious and very fruitful relationship that existed between them at Vatican II itself.

In the light of these attitudes to dissent from Church teaching, and the promotion of the search for fuller truth, it seems right to say that how one reacts to disagreement or dissent is indicative or symbolic of one's whole ecclesiology, of one's model of the Church, and especially of its structures of authority. Those who allow no place for public dissent of a responsible kind seem to be adhering strictly to the institutional model of the Church, and read Vatican II from a Vatican I perspective. The more progressive position sees disagreement as an element in the never-ending search for truth that may be constructive, and helpful to the pilgrim People of God.

Not democracy but democratisation

One sometimes hears it said, especially by more conservative Church people, and not infrequently in response to a call for greater participation in Church life and decisions by the laity and especially by women, that 'the Church is not a democracy'. This statement is, of course, true, but as used in these contexts, and by more institutionally minded Catholics, it tends to carry the meaning that in the Church authority really belongs to the hierarchy, not to the laity and, in particular, not to women; that it is up to those in authority at every level to make the decisions and that, at the end of the day, everyone else is called and indeed obliged to accept and obey these decisions. In short, the meaning conveyed by such an assertion is that the Church is hierarchical to the point that authority is exercised, basically, in a monarchical manner, i.e. by one person who is really the 'boss'.

But, while we would all agree the Church is not formally a

democracy, in the sense in which societies in the Western World are nowadays democracies, there is every reason why, especially in the light of Vatican II, we should seek to develop in the Church what has been called an ethos of democracy. Such an ethos would espouse mutual respect, a readiness of members to make the common interest one's own, to listen to one another, and to ensure that all who are affected by a given decision are accorded a hearing. In a word, a democratic ethos calls for and involves the participation of all, dialogue and open communication at all levels, and participation in all decisions that affect one as a Church member. What is in question here, then, is a process of *democratisation* rather than formal democracy. Such democratisation, in forms of government that are not democracies, envisions the formal enactment of norms of consultation, collaboration, accountability and due process, even in the absence of a mechanism of elections.[3]

One can hardly doubt that the spirit and the letter of Vatican II favours and promotes such a process of democratisation throughout the Church and its structures of authority. It may be added here that in democratic countries there is bound to be pressure on the Church to move in the direction of democratisation, and that this has been and is being resisted inside the Church at every level by powerful forces. However, it is very important for the credibility of the Church in democratic societies that this process of democratisation continue and succeed. An overly monarchical and centralised bureaucracy in the Church distances itself from the faithful and loses contact with urgent pastoral needs. When the Church in and by its structures neglects consultation, collaboration, accountability and due process, and when it assumes an adversarial and negative attitude, then its credibility and its moral authority with its own members *and in society generally* are lessened and gradually eroded.[4] This would seem to be happening at the present time.

Rome and local Churches

Vatican II understood the Church as really a communion of local Churches which together constitute the Church of Christ. This understanding tends to highlight the place and importance of the local Church, and so encourages local initiatives by bishops in their dioceses, by national and regional episcopal conferences, and by the whole local Church in any particular diocese or region. Vatican II's emphasis on collegiality is in line with this renewed significance given to the local Church.

In the light of this, the immediate post-conciliar period (the late 1960s and the early 1 970s) was characterised by the Vatican giving more attention and weight to the voice of local Churches in the appointment of bishops and, as a result, many bishops were ordained who approached their ministry with a Vatican II theology and pastoral attitude. In consequence, a collegial spirit began to percolate through the Church in many dioceses and regions, and great stress came to be placed on pastoral renewal, openness to the signs of the times, and progress in ecumenism. Social justice and the option for the poor became living realities in many local Churches, especially those in Latin America. Overall, the winds of change and growth, so powerfully encouraged by the Council, began to blow refreshingly through the local Church and the Church universal.

In this period, too, the synod of bishops was established and met regularly in Rome, with very significant results, especially in the form of final documents on several important issues, e.g. the priesthood, justice in the world. The synod appeared to be a real and valuable exercise of collegiality between the college of bishops and its head, the Pope. In these years also, national and regional episcopal conferences were set up and proved their value and importance, not merely as forums for discussing issues and exchanging ideas, but also as instruments of teaching and collective decision-making on a range of topics that were of great significance for the local churches of the area. In addition, theologians, continuing the most fruitful relationship between them and the bishops that obtained at Vatican II, did very creative and enriching work on many fronts, while acting also as the best and most probing critics of each other's theological output.

In the last fifteen or more years, however, and especially in the pontificate of John Paul II, a lot of this has changed. There is a definite rowing back from the Vatican II perspectives just mentioned, and we are in the midst of a 'restoration' of pre-Vatican II emphases and attitudes, something that is quite evident in the Vatican's relation to local Churches around the world. The appointment of bishops is, perhaps, the most widely known and debated example. Numerous very conservative bishops have in recent years been appointed, especially to crucial positions in the hierarchy. These bishops place loyalty to the Holy See at the head of their ministerial priorities and are chosen because they are 'safe' men who are judged by Rome to be 'sound', especially on the controversial issues of our day – contraception, the ordination of women and the law of celibacy. These bishops tend to adopt an earlier other-worldly perspective, and to de-emphasise social justice, the option for the poor and the Church's ministry in the political, social and economic areas. All this raises the issue of whether and why individual dioceses should not have a major say in appointing their own bishops, as in the early church, with Rome having, perhaps, a veto. There seems to be no good reason today why this should not be the case.

Add to this the fact that many of these new conservative bishops have been created cardinals and, in consequence, the college of cardinals has now taken on a very restorationist and conservative hue. It appears that the present Pope is preparing the ground for the election of a successor very much in his own image and likeness. Thus, while the language of Vatican II is regularly invoked, there is no doubt that many of its perspectives are less than popular in the Vatican of John Paul II, and seem to have been effectively sidelined.

In relation to the synod of bishops, one has to state with regret that it is now little more than tokenism as far as collegiality is concerned. It is so fully controlled by the Curia that it has only the appearance of being collegial. The bishops of the Church universal air their views on the topic under discussion (itself chosen by Rome), but are not allowed to issue a final document to the Church in general. This is reserved to the Pope who, it seems, incorporates only what suits Vatican policy and thinking at the time. This is greatly to be regretted, since this instrument of collegiality could be a very valuable one, if it were permitted to function in a truly collegial manner. One has to ask, what is the Church's central administration afraid of? Does Peter not trust his fellow bishops to work and speak for the good of the Church in a constructive and helpful way?

We find a similar story in relation to episcopal conferences. In recent times, Cardinal Ratzinger in particular has been endeavouring to establish that these conferences do not have a teaching function. They are, he holds, merely practical instruments for bishops of a particular area to consult together and exchange views, but they do not and cannot teach. Only individual bishops can do that, or a group of bishops in which all have agreed to the statement being made. This seems hard to accept, especially in the light of experience, e.g. the US bishops' pastorals on peace and on economic justice were documents which did in fact teach, even outside the United States, in a very influential way, however much some may seek to deny this. Vatican II speaks of these conferences as places where bishops jointly exercise their pastoral office. Does the Vatican today fear that the magisterium or teaching function of the local Church would somehow take from the papal or curial magisterium, rather than supporting and enhancing it?

The issue of the Vatican silencing or dismissing theologians and removing even bishops from their office is now well known, and, as we have noted, highly controversial. It raises several questions in connection with authority and its structures. The question of respect for the principle of subsidiarity arises here. It seems difficult to accept that these Vatican interventions are fully respectful of it. In addition, one has to wonder whether such methods of suppressing dissent achieve much beyond creating an unhelpful and repressive climate of fear and suspicion. Many have criticised the procedures used as unjust, falling far short of what exists in many secular democracies. One fears that justice within the Church is not attended to with the same zeal and impartiality as Church teaching regularly displays in relation to justice in the world. The 1971 synod of bishops implied as much.

Finally, a recent Vatican document moved from seeing the Church as a communion of local Churches to putting the emphasis again on the universal Church and its leadership, thus highlighting the role of the papacy and the Curia. This de-emphasising of the local Church seems to be central to the thinking and policies at present operative in the Vatican. Until these change, we can only expect more of what the last fifteen years have brought us.

Diocesan structures of authority

The commonest and most talked about structure of authority at diocesan level is the *Council of Priests*. This post-Vatican II institution has been established in most, if not all, dioceses in Ireland and, it would seem, elsewhere also. It is required by Church law (c 495) and is intended to be representative of the presbyterium of the diocese, and to assist the bishop in governance.

One's impression is that, while the Council of Priests does some good work and is in ways a useful structure in a diocese, it is not, generally, viewed with great enthusiasm or approached with deep commitment either by bishops, its priest-members or the clergy of the diocese as a whole. A lot depends on the attitude of the bishop: he may fear it will usurp some of his authority or that he won't be able to control it. He may also be less than enthusiastic about 'democratic' structures and/or may find it difficult to manage or work with such a body. Increasingly today bishops may be less collegially minded, and so more difficulties may arise. In addition, some priests may have a similar mindset. They may not be good at operating collegial structures, may chaff at the time needed to run them well, and feel it's not worth the effort, given the sometimes meagre fruit that results from their work. All this leads on many occasions to a lacklustre Council of Priests that is greatly loved by few, though also seriously disliked by few. There seems to be no easy solution that will make it a really vibrant collegial structure. Both bishops and priests need to change in attitude and commitment and only then will the hopes placed in these councils by Vatican II be fulfilled.

Diocesan synods have been held in some diocese in Ireland with, it would seem, mixed results. Much like the National Pastoral

Congress in England in 1980, the preparation and the synod event itself tend to be truly collegial and even inspirational, though in some places it has degenerated into a bishop-bashing session. The really difficult thing is the follow up or implementation of the synod and its resolutions and decisions. Here the fruits have been thin enough in general and often frustration and anger have been the outcome. How a richer harvest can be garnered in this area is not immediately clear, but one would imagine that a diocesan synod could, in the proper circumstances, and with adequate preparation and structuring, be a very significant event for bishop, priests and laity.

Particularly in the circumstances of the present time in the Irish Church, having a *Diocesan Finance Committee*, as mandated by the Code (c 492), makes eminent sense. How it works in places where it exists will depend a lot on the bishop's openness and commitment to accountability and transparency. One assumes that most dioceses in Ireland do have these committees and that they are valuable collegial structures in and for today's Church.

Another collegial structure that has its roots in Vatican II is what is called the *Diocesan Pastoral Council*. This is quite different from the council of priests and, according to the Code (c 511), may be established' when pastoral circumstances suggest'. It is to be representative of the diocese, priests, religious and especially laity (c 512), and its purpose is to study and weigh those matters which concern pastoral works in the diocese.

One hears relatively little about this kind of instrument of collegiality, at least in Ireland, and one can assume that they have not been established in very many dioceses. What evidence exists points to the conclusion that the performance or success of these pastoral councils has been spotty, much like councils of priests. But it seems fair to state also that pastoral councils can function effectively, if they are encouraged and facilitated in their operation by the bishop and those in other positions of power and influence in the diocese.[5] But here again, old attitudes and styles of leadership and of being led die hard and, hence, many at all levels find it difficult to adjust to and to operate this collegial structure in the spirit it requires for real effectiveness.

We may mention briefly also the position in the diocese that is referred to as the *Vicar Forane* or *Rural Dean*. Some efforts have been made in recent times to revamp this role and the Code (c 555) gives this Vicar some important tasks to carry out, e.g. to promote and coordinate common pastoral action in his vicariate or deanery, to ensure that the liturgy is properly celebrated, the churches well kept and the registers in parishes maintained correctly.

As far as one can observe from experience, VFs, as these functionaries are often called, have a very insignificant role in practice and often do not even attempt to carry out what the Code lays down for them. The reasons for this seem to be that priests generally do not expect or want them to do anything along the lines the Code specifies and VFs themselves seem to take a similar view. The bishop often doesn't encourage a different approach and so VFs end up as virtual non-entities as far as their role is concerned. One feels that there is here room for improvement, so that this structure of authority could be given life and real clout at deanery level. One can say the same thing about the deanery meetings within any particular diocese. Priests seem to feel about these much as they feel about the council of priests and, in consequence, while they do some useful work, they cannot be said to be really successful, at least as far as my experience goes.

One feels that here too diocesan clergy in general are not over-enthusiastic for democratisation within the diocese, at least in practice, perhaps because they find it difficult, haven't got the skills to cope with it, or just prefer the old institutional models and structures at diocesan and, perhaps, also at parish level. Bishops probably feel much the same and so on the ground not a great deal happens and enthusiasm is often lacking. Where collegial structures of authority operate well, one usually finds that it is due to the conviction and energy of individual bishops and/or priests. But unfortunately, such men are relatively scarce.

There is, in general, no structure or system of *accountability* for bishops and for pastoral priests. It must surely be considered a scandal that bishops in diocese and priests in parishes and in other ministries are accountable for their ministry and its quality to no one, except to God through their conscience. Hence, a priest or bishop can be, say, twenty-five years in a parish or diocese or other ministry, can do the minimum, do it badly and with an unhelpful, negative and non-collegial (to put it no stronger) attitude – and very little is or can be done about it. If such a pastor does not fall into heresy or schism, misappropriate parish or diocesan funds, regularly fail to celebrate Mass, or commit some grave misdemeanor like child sex abuse, he can carry on his bad work with scarcely any possibility of anyone doing anything about the situation. Devising a structure of accountability in this regard is not at all easy, but it is urgently needed. Finance committees are, or can be, one element of this accountability; so can liturgy groups and parish councils. But an adequate overall structure does not yet exist.

Another structure of authority that is much needed at diocesan level is some system whereby newly ordained priests are supported and guided in the early years of their ministry. This would help them grow into their new work more easily, avoid many mistakes, cope better with difficulties and failures and, thus, maintain their priestly commitment, self-esteem and good morale at a high level. Something like medical internship might be what is needed here, or at least a pastoral supervision or mentoring system such as obtains in the helping professions in the secular world. One is not, however, optimistic on this score, as very little discussion seems to be taking place among diocesan clergy on these deficiencies in our diocesan pastoral system.

Structures of authority at parish level

At the level of individual parishes one finds that much of what has been said above about dioceses holds true as regards attitudes, collegial structures and their success or lack of it. And perhaps this is not surprising, since at both levels the same priests are involved. Since this is the case, we need look only very briefly at individual pastoral structures within the parish.

In 1980 the National Conference of Priests of Ireland expressed its concern about the general absence of effective *Parish Pastoral*

Councils, and reports from individual diocese confirmed this judgement.[6] Things have probably improved somewhat since then, but one has the impression that a lot still remains to be done in this area, despite strong recommendations and urgings from many bishops. The parish pastoral council is a parish version of the diocesan pastoral council and its purpose is similar. The reasons for its rarity are probably much the same as in the case of councils of priests, and that the attitudes of the laity are not a whole lot different from those of the clergy in relation to such collegial structures.

Other structures at parish level

In some parishes there are many groups or committees working in the pastoral area. They deal with finance, liturgy, religious education, women's issues, youth work, ecumenism, justice questions and so on. At its best a parish can have a great number of such groups. Thus, e.g. Fr Jerry Joyce of Clogh parish, Co Kilkenny tells us that his parish has 36 groups, organisations and services.[7] There are also many other ecclesial groups in existence since Vatican II. Some are parish based and some are not. These too are signs of life or 'seeds of a new Church', as they have been called. Twenty two of them are described in one author's book[8] and they represent a great and rich variety of activities and involvements at the grassroots level of the Church in our day. They are an encouraging and significant fruit of the conciliar renewal that Vatican II initiated and inspired.

Overall, however, one has to admit that at parish level there is a lot more that could be done. Many priests seem to function as basically maintenance men and, so, little happens except the basic sacramental services. These priests are in important ways sacristy or cultic ministers, as priests tended to be in medieval times. Many, perhaps most, laity are happy with this understanding of priesthood and seem not to be tuned in to Vatican II and its theology of the Church, the parish, the priest and the laity. Until this tuning in happens at all levels, the present situation will not change greatly.

Conclusion

What has been said in this chapter will have made it clear that the issue of the Church's structures of authority is a basic one influencing how we view, approach and respond to many specific questions or matters of debate in the life of the Church today. Clearly, one's ecclesiology or understanding of the Church itself has a very pervasive influence on one's position on a whole range of issues, from parish councils to women priests. In a real sense, then, the question of the structures of authority in the Church is the issue behind the issues. Unless we can bridge our differences and arrive at an ecclesiological outlook that brings the conflicting viewpoints into at least a substantial harmony, we are unlikely to get much beyond acrimonious debate, and we will be far from a meeting of minds in regard to what will best promote the welfare of the Church community.

Despite the drive towards 'restoration' that is so powerful in the Church even at the highest level in our day, we can still be grateful for the many seeds of renewal that are growing and bearing fruit at all levels. These represent Vatican II coming to fruition and give grounds for real hope and confidence that the council will, in God's good time, and not ours, produce fruit a hundredfold, in the way Pope John XXIII envisioned and desired.

Notes

1. See Monica Hellwig, *What are the theologians saying now?*, Gill & Macmillan, Dublin, 1992, p 46.

2. Bianchi, Eugene, C., & Radford Ruether, Rosemary, *A Democratic Catholic Church*, Crossroad, NY., 1993, p 34.

3. Coleman, John in *A Democratic Catholic Church*, p 228-9.

4. Coleman, op cit, p 29.

5. Beal, John in *A Democratic Catholic Church*, p 73.

6. *The Furrow*, March & April 1981

7. Joyce, Jerry, *The Laity Help or Hindrance? – A Pastoral Plan*, Mercier Press, 1994, p 86

8. O'Brien, John, CSSp., *Seeds of a New Church*, Columba Press, 1994, Part Two, pp 43-134.

Mosaic or Monolith?

The Appointment of Bishops

Louis McRedmond

For more than a millennium the Church has been faced with the problem of how to ensure the appointment of the most suitable persons as bishops.[1] A great argument in the Middle Ages ended in an uneasy compromise whereby the civil ruler could join in the election of a bishop but only the Pope could 'invest' him: that is, permit him to be consecrated and take charge of his diocese. The Pope could, in theory, veto an inappropriate nominee. In practice, it depended on papal will-power. Some Popes complacently accepted the names put before them, which were often those of clerics wanted by a king or other feudal overlord who had manipulated the election in their favour. Other Popes went to the opposite extreme and made their own nominations without reference to the diocese, which led to the corrupt practice whereby Popes sometimes conferred dioceses on papal officials or other favoured churchmen who might never set foot in the 'local Churches' thus handed them.

The reforms of Trent cleared away much corruption but could not prevent the rulers, now despotic sovereigns of nation states or of conquered nations, from taking an active interest in the appointment of bishops. The quasi-heresy of Gallicanism, rampant in the decades before the French Revolution, evolved as a school of theology to justify the close alliance of 'throne and altar', meaning the government and the bishops, which brought the Church in more than one country perilously close to becoming a State institution as Henry VIII had made it in England and the revolutionaries would try to make it in France. If the Pope failed to assert himself, chief ministers and courtiers could still, until well into the nineteenth century, emerge as bishops and function as senior civil servants or even as politicians. Talleyrand was only the most notorious of these. A later and sadder example was

the Archbishop of Cracow who attempted to influence the con-
clave of 1903, following the death of Leo XIII, by delivering the
Austro-Hungarian Emperor's message demanding that Cardinal
Rampolla be not elected Pope.

The problem throughout was *secular intrusion for secular purposes*
in the appointment process. This was the hazard to be eliminated,
for it obstructed the Church in exercising its right to provide for
its own welfare by choosing its own leaders. The method to be
used by the Church, acting free from secular involvement, was
not definitively laid down. The clergy and laity of a vacant diocese might elect their bishop, as had been the universal practice
in the early Church, or the clergy alone might elect, or the cathedral chapter. Rome might choose of its own volition or might
co-operate with the diocese in making the choice. Without regard to the merits or demerits of any of these approaches, all
were acceptable ways to choose the incoming bishop. What came
to be reserved to Rome in every case was the right to satisfy itself
regarding the procedure employed and the right to assign the
diocese to the person chosen; Rome would indicate its approval
by authorising the bishop's consecration. *Beyond that, no exclus-
ive and inalienable right was asserted for the papacy.*

Through an historical evolution which need not concern us here,
one out of the several acceptable methods of appointment eventually became the norm in the Latin Church. This was, and con-
tinues to be, the practice whereby priests to be made bishops are
chosen by Rome alone, acting often but not always on the advice
of the senior clergy of the diocese in question and the bishops of
the ecclesiastical province to which the diocese belongs.

Regulations were drawn up and incorporated into Church law
to provide in detail the procedure to be followed when an episcopal vacancy occurred. Obviously, the Pope in his plenitude of
power has the authority to adopt this approach. The point to be
grasped is that he does not have to proceed in this way. He can
leave the choice of bishop to the local Church provided that the
system of election has his approval, and that he does not object
to the chosen nominee. He can decide to endorse the decision of
others rather than issue a unilateral directive himself.

The Second Vatican Council went to considerable lengths, both in the Constitution on the Church and in the Decree on Bishops[2], to stress the Pope's authority. But nowhere, not even in the 'explanatory note' attached to the Constitution on the Church to emphasise further the unaltered supremacy of the Pope, was it stated that the entire process of choosing the person to be made bishop of a diocese was solely a function of the Pope. This omission is surely highly significant, given the clear anxiety in the conciliar documents to underscore the extent of papal prerogatives. In fact the Council went beyond silence. It positively recognised that 'the canonical mission of the bishops ... can be made by legitimate customs that have not been revoked by the supreme and universal authority of the Church, or by laws made or acknowledged by the same authority, or directly by Peter's successor himself'. In speaking of the Eastern Churches in union with Rome, it recognised the right of the patriarchs to nominate bishops for these Churches.

Pope Paul VI later issued an instruction on the implementation of the Council's statements regarding bishops. This included a paragraph which, after repeating the Pope's right to nominate, and acknowledging the practice in the Eastern Churches, required episcopal conferences to send the Holy See annually the names of persons suitable for appointment. The whole instruction, however, was described at the outset as dealing with 'matters of discipline'. Accordingly, beyond what the Council had already said, it proposed nothing that was irreversible and not open to discussion.

It may well be asked why the history, the conciliar pronouncements or the papal requirements in connection with the appointment of bishops need to be reflected upon at all. It may be argued that once secular intrusion on appointments has been eliminated, and the Holy See has settled for proceeding by use of its unlimited authority to make dispositions as it chooses, seeking advice but in no way bound by it, the question can be treated as closed. The Church has retrieved total control over appointments. This is what was sought and has now been achieved.

The flaw in this reasoning is that it equates the Church with the papacy. The Church cannot act without, or separated from, the

See of Peter, but the See of Peter can act in ways at variance with the wishes of the rest of the Church or of parts of it. If it does so, its actions will still normally be legitimate: this follows from the fullness of authority with which the papacy is endowed. But authority can be invoked wisely or less wisely. We have no guarantee, outside the narrow bounds of infallibility, that a Pope will always act wisely.

A Pope can make mistakes (again, outside the bounds of infallibility), even in the legitimate exercise of authority with the best intentions and for the good of the Church. Who will argue today that Pius IX acted wisely in publishing the *Syllabus of Errors*, thereby putting the Church in a bind from which it took a century to extricate itself? Or that Pius X was wise in the comprehensiveness with which he condemned modernism, and as a result caused anguish to many faithful Catholics and sparked fear or scrupulosity in others? We can voice misgivings about those papal actions today. But, in the phrase of a recent billboard advertisement, where is the comfort in that? How much more useful if misgivings can be voiced when mistakes seem to be happening and can be redressed? To voice misgivings about a papal action is not to be disloyal, for it does not reject papal authority. On the contrary, it implicitly accepts papal authority by showing concern that it be exercised in the most beneficial way. Criticism from within the Church contributes to the mind of the Church and thus collaborates with, rather than opposes, the papacy by putting forward considerations for the papacy to take into account in the ongoing government of the Church in ever-changing society.

The appointment of bishops falls into the category of what is debatable by loyal Catholics because of the history, conciliar statements and papal attitudes outlined above. Invalid ways of appointment have been identified, i.e. by secular intervention or without papal approval. A sole and only way has not been defined. It follows that the way at present employed for the Latin Church, although legitimate, is not the only way possible. This automatically creates room to examine whether another way might not be better. To raise that question implies misgivings about the present approach. Are there grounds for such misgiv-

ings? In part, the answer consists of observable experience – the
evidence before us – and, in part, of reflection on the nature of
the bishop's role in the Church.

Some contentious appointments

The evidence, it must immediately be said, suggests that a number, perhaps many, appointments are in fact being made in line
with the recommendations of the local Church, or at least of the
local clergy, as mediated through the diocesan chapter or similar
body and the bishops of the ecclesiastical province. Such appointments are normally welcomed by the faithful of the diocese. Unfortunately, another approach has been taken so often in
recent years that the local Church has again and again been divided, alienated, angered by the appointment. This always is a
case in which the Holy See has named as bishop somebody un-
known to the diocese or, if known, somebody whose priorities
or way of thinking conflicts with the perceived needs of the diocese, as its people understand them. He may be a good and holy
man but is seen to lack sympathy with – that is, sensitivity to –
the Church delivered into his care.

Thus in the 1970s the Catholic Church in the Netherlands, which
had been to the fore in helping to formulate the mind of the
Second Vatican Council and afterwards in giving effect to its
major teachings, had bishop after bishop of radically different
and deeply conservative views imposed upon it: Adriaan
Simonis in Rotterdam (and later, as cardinal, in Utrecht), Jan
Matthijs Gijsen in Roermond, Hendrik Bomers in Haarlem.
Attempts by such bishops to reverse the direction being taken
by the Dutch Church caused deep demoralisation among a people who felt themselves condemned by Rome for their enthusiastic commitment to conciliar reform.[3] Mass attendance fell
sharply, as did vocations, and much of the remaining enthusiasm for progress in line with the Council became channelled
into the 'Eighth of May' movement, set up and promoted without episcopal approval – yet ironically claiming to represent
those 'who now carry the torch in succession to Alfrink', a reference to the famous Dutch cardinal who had been a towering influence at Vatican II.

Something similar happened in Austria in the 1980s. The appointment of Bishops Kurt Krenn to St Pölten, Georg Eder to Salzburg and especially of Hans Groër to Vienna (upon the retirement of the Alfrink-like Cardinal Koenig), all sparked resentment similar to that in the Netherlands. What happened was even more remarkable, for the Austrian Church lacked the popular zeal for reform which emerged in Holland after the Council. As Catholics either apathetic towards religion or traditionally pious, the Austrians could have been expected to accept the bishops chosen for them by Rome with no more than puzzlement or a grumble of discontent. The grumbling was there from the outset, but might have grown no louder had these pastors not complacently played down the problems of conscience, the feminist issues, the difficulty for priests in observing celibacy, and the other questions common to the Church in Western society today. What caused distress was not that they refused to adopt what conservatives would consider the 'liberal agenda'. It seems to have been rather that they showed no concern for the pressures felt by their people, and thought it sufficient to respond by repeating the Roman denunciations of the world in which their people lived: they brought neither consolation nor good tidings.

The result was the extraordinary eruption of protest through a referendum in 1995 . More than 50 per cent of Austria's practising Catholics declared their support for reforms whereby the teaching Church could be seen to listen and respond, in a caring way, to the anxieties of Catholics living their faith in the modern world. In this context they favoured the abolition of compulsory priestly celibacy, a more understanding approach on sexual morality, the ordination of women and much else. But in the first place, 'right in the forefront' according to Father Paul Zulehner, Professor of Pastoral Theology at Vienna University, was the demand for a new approach to the appointment of bishops. Most respondents, not only among those who supported the protest but also the majority of those who opposed it, wanted both the priests and laity in the local Church to be involved in the nomination of candidates for appointment. In Austria this was judged the major outcome of the referendum. It was noted that the protest received more than average support in dioceses where the bishop was one of those imposed by Rome with no apparent regard for local wishes. The clear message was that such wishes should be the determining factor for Rome.[4]

Bewilderment, pain and a sense of outrage has marked the reaction to appointments in a number of other countries too. In Switzerland half the cathedral chapter refused to attend the consecration of Bishop Wolfgang Haas of Chur in 1988[5], and in 1991 Catholics in Lucerne organised a remonstrance complaining, among other matters, that bishops were being appointed 'without any consultation of the faithful, let alone with their codetermination'.[6] A report from the Philippines in 1990[7] spoke of disquiet among the priests of a diocese where they felt their new bishop was betraying everything his predecessor had stood for. In 1995 in San Salvador 200 laity protested to Rome over the appointment of Archbishop Saenz Lacalle to the see once occupied by Archbishop Romero: they could not, they said, 'discern the presence of the Holy Spirit in the choice' which conflicted with the local desire for a pastor known to be committed to 'the search for peace with justice in El Salvador'.[8] The next month, another report from Central America forecast 'passive resistance' towards the new archbishop of Mexico City[9], while Dom Helder Camera, the retired Archbishop of Olinda-Recife in Brazil, has had to watch his Rome-chosen but locally unasked-for successor, Dom Jose Sobrinho, dismantle most of his initiatives for combating poverty and social injustice: here, as in Holland, a lay group committed itself to carrying on some of the work without episcopal approval.[10]

Signs of unity?

To all of these reports, as well as the less dramatic stories which can be told about the rejection by Rome of local wishes regarding some Irish appointments in recent years[11], the irrelevant answer will tiresomely be made that the Church is not a democracy. Nobody said it was. But the Vatican Council said that bishops 'are the visible source and foundation of unity in their own particular Churches'. Of *unity*. If the appointment of a bishop is seen to be the cause of dissension, protest, alienation of clergy or laity or both, he is a visible foundation of *dis*unity. It may not be his fault, since he must be true to his conscience and to his own vision of his calling, and this integrity may inevitably lead him into conflict with his people if their vision is otherwise. Responsibility, however, can scarcely be avoided by whoever did the appointing, if the focus of division and revolt in a diocese is the person appointed to be the focus of unity. An occasional misjudgment would be humanly understandable. A consistent pattern of appointments resulting in serious disunity is another matter.

As we have seen, the appointing is done by the Pope. Any Pope will, of course, be conscious that, just as the bishop is meant to be the focus of unity in the diocese, the Pope is meant to be the focus of unity in the universal Church. A special aspect of that unity is the relationship of the Pope with the bishops collectively. The Pope and bishops together constitute what the Council called 'the college or body of bishops' who are 'the expression of ... the unity of the flock of Christ, in so far as it is assembled under one head'. It would be humanly understandable if a Pope were to wish this unity to be made visible through a body of bishops of one mind with himself. But is it reasonable to expect that kind of unity? Would it even be the kind of unity envisaged by the Council?

At a time of flux and change in the Church as well as in human society, it is scarcely surprising that bishops should differ among themselves on many questions not of faith or morals, or, even if of faith or morals, open to further refinement of interpretation and explanation. Each bishop will be conditioned by his background, his intellectual tendency, his experience, the part of the world in which he lives, the needs of his people as he understands them, his spiritual priorities arrived at through prayer and reflection. With such a wide basis for differences of viewpoint, any Pope will inevitably find himself in disagreement on a number of questions with a number of bishops. To some extent, no doubt varying with successive holders of the supreme office, the Pope will see disunity in this divergence of opinion and attitude. When vacancies arise we may assume that a Pope concerned to mitigate disunity a little will be happier to see these vacancies filled by bishops close to his way of thinking instead of conspicuously otherwise.

This is to speak tentatively of what might be expected. In fact it is common case that a more robust determination has taken hold in Rome so that, in the 1980s and the 1990s to date, priests who are less than rigid in their support of the ban on artificial contraception in the encyclical *Humanae Vitae*, or who preach liberation theology, or who favour removal of compulsory celibacy for priests, are unlikely now to be appointed bishops[12]. It is unnecessary here to examine the merits or deficiencies of these questions, beyond noting the ample grounds to suppose that firm allegiance to prevailing Roman attitudes on a variety of contentious subjects is frequently sought by the Vatican today in candidates for episcopal appointment. Equally ample grounds exist to support the contention that dioceses whose bishops have long been prominently committed to alternative attitudes are destined to receive a successor in due course who will dedicate himself to eradicating the elements of diocesan activity offensive to Roman thinking which he finds *in situ* on his arrival.

An Irish Precedent

Ireland, as it happens, provides an interesting example remote in time which shows a papalist stance similar to that now in evidence and which has had an instructive outcome in our own day.[13] When Paul Cullen returned to Ireland in 1850 not only as Archbishop of Armagh and Primate but also as Papal Delegate, which effectively gave him administrative authority over the Irish Church, he was horrified by the division of opinion among the bishops on the then topical controversy regarding the Queen's Colleges. The question was whether these nondenominational university institutions being set up in Belfast, Cork and Galway by the British government were suitable places of learning for Catholic students. Cullen emphatically opposed them and had persuaded Pope Pius IX to endorse his criticism, but some 11 Irish bishops persisted in their view that the colleges would meet the pressing educational needs of the Catholic community.

Cullen's description of this attitude was 'Gallican'. It was an unhappy abuse of language for what it implied was that the bishops were allied with the government to advance government policy. In reality, as is crystal clear from all they said and wrote at the time, they simply wanted to achieve what they believed to be best for their people. But the Primate was convinced that any disagreement with Rome was disloyal rebellion, even on a pragmatic issue like the merit or otherwise of a particular university. There was only one solution, as Cullen saw it. He wrote to the appropriate curial cardinal: 'If the Sacred Congregation will take great care in the choice of new bishops, within three years the condition of things will be totally changed in Ireland'. He kept hammering out this message. Of his favoured candidate for a vacant diocese: 'He is well disposed to be obedient to the Holy See, and this is a quality which for the future ought to be required in every new bishop in Ireland'; of appointments in general: 'We want our new bishops to be orthodox in everything, but especially devoted to the Holy See'. And so on.

What happened then and later, when Cullen had become Archbishop of Dublin and cardinal, is a complex story but can be readily summarised. The formidable churchman got his way, by and large got the bishops he wanted, and thereby achieved a unanimity of viewpoint posited on that comprehensive concurrence with Roman attitudes for which Rome itself thirsted in those days of rampant anticlericalism. The seeming unity of the Irish bishops with one another, and of the hierarchy with the Holy See on every issue, great or small, survived for some 140 years. At the time of writing (1995), however, episcopal unanimity has been shown to be a facade. Bishops have differed in public over whether the rule of compulsory celibacy in the Latin Church should be open to discussion[14]. Those who argue for discussion have been reproved because they dare to say what the Holy See does not wish to be said. The 1850s echo loudly, and questions must now be asked which perhaps should have been asked then.

Unity or uniformity?

The essential question, already being wisely put in Ireland, is whether uniformity must be considered a necessary component of unity[15]. Rome and the more ardent apologists of papal authority seem to think so, as their predecessors did in 1850. The Second Vatican Council took a radically different view. It saw the college of bishops as 'the expression of the multifariousness and universality of the People of God' and said that the 'multiplicity of local Churches, unified in a common effort, shows all the more resplendently the catholicity of the undivided Church'. As to the bishops themselves, each 'represents his own Church, whereas all, together with the Pope, represent the whole Church'; they were to collaborate with one another and with the Pope, but were not 'to be regarded as vicars of the Roman Pontiff; for they exercise the power which they possess in their own right'.

The Council went on to give some practical directives. Bishops were to be 'solicitous for all the churches' and especially 'for those parts of the world ... in which, especially on account of the scarcity of priests, the faithful are in danger of falling away'. They were to present doctrine 'in a manner suited to the needs of the times, that is, so it may be relevant to those difficulties and questions which men find especially worrying and intimidating'. And since the Church was to relate closely to the society in which she lived, bishops were 'to approach men and to initiate and promote dialogue with them'.

What we have here is surely the unity of a mosaic, not of a monolith. Bishops are certainly to represent Rome to their people, but equally they are to represent their people to Rome. Dialogue involves listening as well as speaking; concern for people's difficulties in the modern world can spring only from a sympathetic understanding of what worries them; to have a care for the Church elsewhere means reflecting on its problems and how they might be relieved. Such interaction by each bishop with the world around him and beyond him contributes to his own perception of present circumstances and of what the Church should be doing about them. This perception is his contribution to the mind of the Church, his piece of the mosaic. With each from his own standpoint bringing forward his own perception, each inevitably different in some degree from the rest, the whole picture can be built up under the Pope's direction. The projection of the whole picture in turn is the Church's message to the world of our times, its part of the dialogue, conveyed by its bishops. This is the unity envisaged by the Council, a unity created out of multifariousness, multiplicity, *catholicity*.

Such unity can clearly embrace an Irish bishop who wants celibacy discussed because of its relevance to the shortage of priests, a Latin American bishop who finds a coincidence between certain features of Marxism and gospel exhortations on justice for the poor, an Austrian or Dutch bishop who thinks that Church teaching on sexual morality needs to be expanded to take account of developments in modern society. None of these bishops can be easily accommodated in the latter-day papalist concept of unity, since their perceptions clash with those of Rome. It follows that priests known to share their perceptions have little prospect of being appointed bishops, even if put forward in the due process of the *ternus*, the proposal of three names by the senior clergy of the vacant diocese for consideration by Rome. The equation of unity with unanimity means that the very diversity which the Vatican Council saw as the warp and woof of the bishops' relationship with the Holy See is a suspect factor to be kept out of the episcopacy, if detected in time in a candidate for appointment.

The role of the Nuncio

Unwanted traits can be identified in Rome through the involvement of the Papal Nuncio in the appointment of bishops. The nuncio is not only the Vatican ambassador accredited to the state but is also the Papal Legate to the local Church. Canon 377.3 of the Code of Canon Law says that when a *ternus* is being prepared the Papal Legate must 'seek individually' the views of certain bishops and clergy in the ecclesiastical province to which the vacant diocese belongs. It goes on: 'If he judges it expedient, he is also to seek individually, and in secret, the opinions of other clerics ... and of lay people of outstanding wisdom.' He is to send their advice 'together with his own opinion' to the Holy See. While the mandatory veil of secrecy hides the precise details of a nuncio's contribution to the selection of any one bishop, enough is known to leave little doubt that his comments on the names in a *ternus* carry considerable weight in Rome, and may operate to exclude all of them from being considered. Equally,

'his own opinion' may bring about the appointment of somebody unthought of by the local Church, and of a mentality un-
welcome to its clergy and laity.

A remarkable pointer to the role played by a nuncio is the re-
ported claim by Monsignor Gaetano Alibrandi, who served as
nuncio to Ireland for twenty years, that his recommendations on
episcopal appointments were always accepted by Rome; he also
said that *he allowed* several Irish bishops to stay in office until
they reached the age of eighty.[16] It seems extraordinary that
such extensive influence, in matters of outstanding importance
to the local Church, should be permitted to a mere clerico-diplo-
matic official, but the suspected power of a nuncio can be sensed
as well in complaints like those more recently heard in Mexico
City, where the new archbishop was thought to be the choice of
the nuncio there, and in San Salvador, where the protesting laity
wrote to the Vatican to denounce the 'decisive intervention' of
the nuncio to their country in a similar case.[17] In fairness, it
should be added that a nuncio's discreet comments could be
helpful if the local hierarchy were functioning under improper
pressures (perhaps in a totalitarian State), so that their advice
was not to be trusted. But these would be highly exceptional circumstances which it would be ludicrous to invoke when determining procedures to be applied as the norm throughout the
Catholic world.

The norm should surely be governed by rational considerations.
A nuncio may advise well or badly, depending on whom he
consults (which is never made public). His own inclinations
must also, humanly speaking, play a part. His knowledge of
Roman policy – the kind of bishops Rome wants – may reasonably be assumed to be his primary concern: after all, he represents Rome, not the local Church. The last fact is surely what
should be of greatest concern. Whether a nuncio acts wisely or
otherwise is not really the issue. The question is rather why he
should be involved at all. The answer can be put as a further
question in down-to-earth terms. Who is likely to know best the
needs of a diocese? The people who live and work there? Or a
delegate sent from Rome? Or for that matter, the Vatican

Congregation for Bishops which will normally act for the Pope in making the ultimate decision?

To give the obvious answer to the basic question does not challenge the authority of Rome. It simply tells Rome by whose advice it should be guided. If the advice of the local Church is rejected because it would result in the appointment of a person with opinions out of favour in Rome, we have to conclude that Roman views are receiving priority over the people's needs, or at least that Rome believes itself better able to judge their needs than the people themselves. The age in which we live does not look with favour on such paternalism in any aspect of human life, for the rule of despots, even benevolent despots, has too often been marked by error, frustration, turmoil and misery. But however persuasive this may be as a practical consideration, we need not pursue it to the point where it provokes the predictable rejoinder that the Church is not a democracy. There is another, more compelling case to be made.

We need only recall the Second Vatican Council's vision of Church to see how inadequate is the imposition on all of a unilateral perception from the centre, and how the Church itself is emasculated if its local leaders are chosen to represent Rome rather than the diocese which they govern. Contributions of thought, experience, example and concern from the periphery cannot be gathered in; worse, they are discouraged by bishops for whom difference from Rome is dangerous and devious. The multifariousness of the People of God is thus rejected as of no value. The collegiality of bishops becomes increasingly meaningless, as more and more bishops have no message to bring to the centre other than what the centre has predetermined they will bring. And all for what? A fictitious unity, an illusion like the unanimity of Irish bishops who, as we now know, harbour an adult diversity of opinion too long concealed from their people. The Church does not lose its multitudinous character because diversity is painted over. But the pieces of the mosaic are left unassembled. In practical terms, this means that *some only* of the issues facing the Church, *some only* of the obstacles to the preaching and practice of the gospel, are dealt with ... and dealt with by *some only* of the relevant criteria.

The manner in which bishops are chosen is crucial to the restoration of the Church in all its life-giving diversity. As a minimum requirement, the bishop must be sensitive to the concerns of those to whom he is sent. If he shares these concerns, so much the better. If he can be found already sharing these concerns within the diocese, best of all. Of course, other qualities will also be sought, from competence in leadership to personal godliness, but what must be a *sine qua non* is the inclination and ability *to represent his own Church*, as the Council said – that is, to re-present it; to present its thoughts, its values, its experience, its activity, its hopes and its anxieties, in the wider forum of the universal Church and, again, to bear all these in mind with sympathy and understanding when he speaks to his own people as their pastor.

To find such a bishop it is vital that the local Church be heard, for only the local Church knows precisely what kind of person will meet its needs. Canon 377.1. indicates how this might be done, when it says that 'the Supreme Pontiff freely appoints bishops *or confirms those lawfully elected*' (author's italics). An election is therefore possible. It is surely desirable. The mechanism may vary but ideally should involve laity as well as clergy, perhaps through a pastoral council. There is no evident reason why it should involve an intermediary between the local Church and Rome, except insofar as someone may be needed to receive and convey the feeling of the diocese. Thereafter it is for the Pope, using what agencies he thinks appropriate, to make the final decision. In that he cannot be fettered. But if the spirit of the Council is to prevail, the only questions to be asked on his behalf will be those necessary to establish that due process has been observed. Local wishes can then be allowed to prevail and the universal Church can be enriched by a new pastor appointed to pick up and burnish and put in place that stone of the mosaic consigned to his care. As Pope Leo the Great put it: 'He who has the trust of the clergy and the people should become bishop.'[18]

Notes

1. The historical summary which follows draws largely on Henri Daniel Rops: *History of the Church of Christ*, vol 3, chapters V and VI; vol 9, chapter II.

2. Quotations throughout this essay from the Dogmatic Constitution on the Church, the Decree on the Pastoral Office of Bishops in the Church and the instruction of Paul VI referred to in the text are taken from *Vatican Council II: the Conciliar and Post Conciliar Documents*, General Editor: Austin Flannery, O.P., Dominican Publications, Dublin.

3. See 'Rome's bulldozer' by Walter Goddijn, *The Tablet*, 23 February 1991.

4. See 'Respectable revolt' by Paul Zulehner, *The Tablet*, 29 July 1995.

5. *The Tablet*, 28 May 1988, p 630.

6. *The Tablet*, 30 March 1991, p 416.

7. Dunn, Joseph, *No Lions in the Hierarchy*, The Columba Press, Dublin, p 257.

8. *The Tablet*, 29 July 1995, p 980.

9. *The Tablet*, 5 August 1995, p 1008.

10. See 'A vision destroyed' by Peter Stanford, *The Tablet*, 22 July 1995. Also see Dunn, op cit, pp 254-255.

11. For Irish questioning of Roman methods, see *The Tablet*, 5 September 1987, pp 942-943.

12. See Dunn, op cit, pp 260-263.

13. The factual material in the historical summary which follows is taken from Emmet Larkin: *The Making of the Roman Catholic Church in Ireland*, 1850-1860.

14. See reports in *The Sunday Tribune*, 11 and 24 June 1995, and *The Irish Times*, 13 and 28 June 1995.

15. See 'True Church unity does not depend on uniformity' by Seán MacRéamoinn, *The Irish Times*, 20 July 1995.

16. See interview with Monsignor Alibrandi by John Cooney, *The Irish Press*, 10, 11 and 12 October 1994, and Dunn, op cit, p 28.

17. *The Tablet*, 29 July and 5 August 1995, loc cit, (above).

18. *The Tablet*, 2 September 1995, p 1122, quoting Bishop Rheinhold Stecher of Innsbruck (Austria).

PART II

Alternative Models

Authority in the Church of Ireland

Catherine McGuinness

The basic law and structure of the Church of Ireland, as in the case of the Republic of Ireland, is set out in a written constitution. As in the case of *Bunreacht na hÉireann*, the constitution of the Church of Ireland starts with a Preamble. (So far, however, no one has suggested that all references to God should be removed from it!) The 'Preamble and Declaration', to give it its correct title, is of fundamental importance to the Church and is quoted, referred to and relied upon on many occasions. It is, I consider, worth quoting a number of its major sections fully:

'In the Name of the Father, and of the Son and of the Holy Ghost. Amen: whereas it hath been determined by the Legislature that on and after the first day of January 1871 the Church of Ireland shall cease to be established by law; and that the ecclesiastical law of Ireland shall cease to exist as law save as provided in the 'Irish Church Act 1869' and it hath thus become necessary that the Church of Ireland should provide for its own regulation:

We, the Archbishops and Bishops of this Ancient Catholic and Apostolic Church of Ireland, together with the representatives of the Clergy and laity of the same in General Convention assembled in Dublin in the year of Our Lord God 1870, before entering on this work, do solemnly declare as follows:

1. The Church of Ireland doth as heretofore accept and unfeignedly believe all the Canonical Scriptures of the Old and New Testament as given by inspiration of God and containing all things necessary to salvation; and doth continue to profess the faith of Christ as professed by the Primitive Church.

2. The Church of Ireland will continue to minister the doctrine and sacraments and the discipline of Christ as the Lord hath commanded and will maintain inviolate the three orders of bishops, priests or presbyters, and deacons in the sacred ministry ....

The Church of Ireland deriving its authority from Christ, Who is the Head over all things to the Church, doth declare that a General Synod of the Church of Ireland, consisting of the Archbishops and Bishops and of representatives of the clergy and laity shall have chief legislative power therein, and such administrative power as may be necessary for the Church and consistent with its episcopal constitution.'

The Preamble and Declaration also affirms 'the reformed and protestant' nature of the Church of Ireland, approves the 39 Articles and the Book of Common Prayer of 1662 and declares that the Church of Ireland will maintain communion with the Church of England and all other Christian Churches agreeing in the principles of the Preamble and Declaration.

The Church of Ireland is, then, an independent Church where power and authority are exercised by the General Synod in a manner 'consistent' with the episcopal constitution of the Church. In many ways, the system set up in 1870 was a revolutionary one and represented a historic change in the way in which the Church of Ireland, which had before then been an established or State Church was governed. The system of self-government under the General Synod has by and large worked extremely well and is, I think, one of the great strengths of the Church of Ireland. Perhaps I should emphasise here – because from time to time I hear mistaken assertions on the subject made in political and other circles – that the Church of Ireland is in no way subject to the authority of the Church of England and that the British Monarch is not in any sense the Head of the Church of Ireland.

As in the case of the Roman Catholic Church, the Church of Ireland is organised into parishes which are grouped in dioceses, each diocese or group of dioceses having a bishop. However, the general distribution of authority within the Church is very different. I propose here to summarise the actual structure of authority and then to make a few comments on the way in which it has been exercised, its strengths and weaknesses.

Under the Church of Ireland parochial system, Ireland is divided into parishes which are land areas; there may be unions of parishes or there may be grouped parishes. Each parish will have an *Incumbent* or *Rector* and may also have one or more curates, more correctly called *curates assistant*. As far as organisation is concerned, the basic unit is the 'registered vestry men' (and women) of the parish who constitute the *General Vestry*. These are members of the Church of Ireland over 18 years of age who are either parishioners of the parish, or accustomed members of the congregation for the previous three months, or the owners of landed or house property situated within the parish of the clear yearly value of at least £10. In my experience, the third category does not arise frequently for practical purposes. The General Vestry meets once a year shortly after Easter. Its chief duty is to carry out various selections but it also may have the parochial accounts presented to it and often has some general discussion with regard to the business of the parish. However, its actual powers are strictly limited. For instance, it elects the *Select Vestry* of twelve persons, but it cannot try to censor or overrule them. As in the case of elections to the Dáil, if the General Vestry, as a whole, disapproves of the actions of the Select Vestry, its only remedy is to throw them out and elect a new vestry the following year.

The General Vestry also elects one *Church Warden* – generally known as the 'People's Church Warden' and also a '*Glebe Warden*'. The Rector of the parish also appoints a Church Warden and a Glebe Warden. Every three years, the General Vestry also elect members of the parish to represent it at the *Diocesan Synod,* and *Parochial Nominators* who have a role in appointing a new Rector where there is a vacancy . Generally speaking, the duties of the Select Vestry are to have charge of the Church funds, to keep the Church and other parochial buildings in a proper state of repair and to have them insured, and to provide for everything necessary for the worship of the Church, such as books, furniture, communion vessels and linen, baptismal and burial registers, and so on. Church Wardens keep the register of vestrymen, maintain order during Divine Service and have a number of other functions. In practice, the Church Wardens take a leading part in assisting the Rector in the running of the Church Services and other parochial matters. The Glebe Wardens look after the parish property.

The Rector or Incumbent is appointed by a Board of Nomination which consists of the bishop or archbishop of the diocese, the four Parochial Nominators elected by the General Vestry, and four clergy and one lay person representing the diocese. Once he is appointed, the rector has reasonable security of tenure and holds office until he either resigns or dies. At present, rectors must retire at the age of 70. A rector cannot otherwise be removed without his consent, except in accordance with a resolution of the diocesan synod (which is approved by the bishop) that there is no longer sufficient work in the parish to justify its continued existence as a separate benefice, or as a result of a decision of the Court of the General Synod. Thus it can be seen that in the Church of Ireland the priest in charge of a parish cannot be moved simply at the will of the bishop. This right has sometimes been referred to as 'the parson's freehold' and in practice the power of removing a rector without his consent has not been operated for many years. However, the parson's freehold is not an inalienable right, as it depends on the relevant provisions of the Constitution of the Church and can be altered by a statute of the General Synod as, for instance, when a compulsory retirement age was introduced. Curates assistant, however, are appointed by the bishop, generally on the nomination of the rector, and may be moved from post to post by the bishop.

It will be seen from this that the ordinary parishioners have quite a considerable authority and power within the parish, although of course their power is mainly confined to practical matters of administration. They have, however, the power of the purse, since the parish's finances are controlled by the Select Vestry and the Parish Treasurer, and parish accounts are presented to the parish each year in what is now frequently called an 'open and transparent' manner. The spiritual direction of the parish is of course in the hands of the rector, who may sometimes appoint a pastoral council to assist him is this field. However, such councils have no authority as such within the Church structure. Difficulties can of course arise out of the operation of this balance of power in a parish, particularly where there may be some disagreement between a rector and a Select Vestry. In my experience, however, this does not occur very often and is generally limited to a certain amount of normal grumbling on both sides. Operating the system, however, does require a certain amount of administrative skill on the part of a rector, and I feel that in the training of clergy perhaps a little more attention might be given to this aspect, particularly some training in the chairing of meetings; the most saintly and spiritual man may after all be not particularly skilled in organisation and administration, and may indeed be a very poor chairperson.

As far as diocesan organisation is concerned, the Church of Ireland is divided into two provinces, the province of Armagh and the province of Dublin. Each province has an archbishop and within the provinces, each diocese has a bishop. Again, authority within the diocese is distributed between the bishop, the clergy and the laity. The basic structure is the Diocesan Synod which consists of the bishop, the clergy of the diocese and lay members of the synod. As I have already said, the lay members of the diocesan synod are elected by the General Vestry of each parish every three years, and any communicant lay member of the Church of Ireland aged over 18 is eligible for election. The Diocesan Synod itself decides the number of lay synod members to be elected for each parish, but there must be not less than two and not more than five lay synod members for each clergyman normally officiating in the parish. This means that there are, by and large, at least twice as many lay members of the Diocesan Synod as there are clergy. The Diocesan Synod must meet once a year and generally this is its only meeting. At this meeting, it elects a Diocesan Council which again consists of clergy and lay people and is presided over by the bishop. The Diocesan Council carries out the general business of the diocese during the year.

At the meeting of the Diocesan Synod, the Diocesan Council reports to it and there are usually reports from a number of other committees. Individual members may also bring motions in much the same way as motions are brought before either House of the Oireachtas. Every three years the Diocesan Synod elects clerical and lay members from the diocese for the General Synod, and also elects episcopal electoral representatives who play a part in the election of the bishop of the diocese. The annual meeting of the Diocesan Synod is an important occasion in the life of the diocese, and usually begins with a Presidential address by the bishop in which he takes the opportunity to comment both on the general work of the diocese and also, frequently, on matters of general public interest to the members of the Church of Ireland. For instance, in the Dublin diocese in recent years the archbishop has taken the opportunity to refer to the somewhat vexed question of the Adelaide Hospital and the move to Tallaght, and this has been discussed with some passion at the synod.

In each diocese there is also an archdeacon who is appointed by the bishop. The Constitution sets out that 'it is the duty and office of an archdeacon from ancient times to aid and assist the bishop in his pastoral care and office. He is at all times to watch, enquire, and report whatever may need the consideration and control of the bishop and more especially when the bishop may direct him to make enquiry ....' This might suggest to the suspicious mind that the archdeacon was a kind of spy for the bishop, and this may have been so from time to time in the past, but in my own experience I have never seen an archdeacon act in this way. In general he is a useful assistant to the bishop in the administration of the diocese.

I should perhaps here deal with the method of election of bishops. For this purpose there are two episcopal electoral colleges, one for the province of Armagh and one for the province of Dublin. The electoral college consists of the archbishop or the senior bishop of the province and three other bishops, together with twelve clerical and twelve lay electoral representatives from the vacant diocese. In the province of Armagh, there are also two clerical and two lay electoral representatives from each of the other dioceses in the province. In the province of Dublin there are three clerical and three lay representatives from each other diocese in the province. There are therefore 52 people on the electoral college, whose proceedings are of course confidential. It is provided that the electoral college should first have an informal discussion as to the needs of the diocese, and the type of person who might best suit the appointment as bishop. After that, proposals may be made of the name of any bishop or priest of not less than 30 years of age. Voting is by orders – that is the clergy vote together and the laity vote together, and it requires a two-thirds majority of both orders to elect a bishop. If this cannot be achieved, then the right of election passes to the House of Bishops. I think it would be true to say that most electoral colleges make every effort to avoid this outcome.

As in the case of rectors, therefore, it can be seen that there is a high degree of ordinary lay participation in the selection of bishops. The only exception to this rule is that the Archbishop of Armagh, who is the Primate of all Ireland, is elected by the House of Bishops from among its own number. A bishop can only be removed by a decision of the Court of the General Synod, but he must retire at the age of 70.

As is set out in the Preamble, the central authoritative body in the Church of Ireland is the General Synod, which consists of two Houses, the House of Bishops and the House of Representatives. The clerical and lay members of the House of Representatives are elected every three years by the diocesan synods, and the number of seats is allocated between the diocese in accordance with their Church population. There is a total of 648 members, so it is a large and sometimes rather unwieldly body. Again, there are roughly twice as many lay members as clerical members. It meets for three days in May of each year, traditionally in Dublin, but recently twice in Belfast and once in Cork. The two main aspects of its work are the continuation and enactment of legislation, and the presentation and debate of reports from the various committees. Bills are debated and passed in stages in a very similar way to that used in the Houses of the Oireachtas. The General Synod may by statute amend the Constitution of the Church – I am rather thankful to say that it is not necessary to hold a referendum! The General Synod is presided over by

the Primate, the Archbishop of Armagh, and he also addresses
the Synod at the beginning of each session. Again he will use
this address to deal both with specifically Church matters and
also with matters of interest to the general public. Like the diocesan synods, the General Synod is open to the public and to the
press, although it may occasionally have a closed session.

At the risk of being irreverent, I would suggest that the General
Synod in many ways is comparable to an Ard-Fheis or Party
Conference. It is an occasion for the delegates to meet and so-
cialise and to create solidarity. It has also, it seems to me, played
a considerable part in preventing a split developing between the
members of the Church living in Northern Ireland and those living in the Republic, and has promoted some measure of understanding between them – although there can also be quite a high
degree of political disagreement among the speakers.

As regards the membership, the rules of election ensure that there
is a reasonably wide spread among the age groups, although as
in all bodies of this type, there is a preponderance of the middle-
aged. Women have been eligible for election to all administrative bodies in the Church for many years. But while there is a
goodly proportion of women in the General Synod, they are still
considerably in a minority, as the vast majority of clergy are still
male. However, it is somewhat remarkable, if not surprising,
that women are in a very small minority on the two most powerful administrative entities in the Church – the Standing Committee of the General Synod, and the representative Church
body. In 1995, there were three women out of a membership of
sixty in the representative Church body, which is the trustee
which holds the property and investments of the Church and ex-
ercises considerable financial power. The Standing Committee is
the executive body of the Synod which carries on its business
during the year. In 1994 eight members out of sixty-eight were
women and, by 1995, this had decreased to eight out of seventy-
one. The increase in membership was caused by the fact that one
co-opted member – a woman – resigned and was replaced by
four men! I should say, however, that the women members of
the General Synod are active members who contribute frequently
to the debates.

It might be said that the matters dealt with by the General Synod are largely structural, administrative and financial and that much of the spiritual and theological authority remains in the hands of the bishops. However, this would not be altogether true. For example, it is through the General Synod that the major modernisation and revision of the liturgy contained in the Book of Common Prayer has been carried out over the last twenty years. Another example would be the long discussion in the Synod as to whether divorced persons could be remarried in Church and if so, under what conditions. Perhaps the best example of all is the decision to ordain, firstly, women deacons and, later, women priests. This was a very important change in the practice of the Church of Ireland and was considered over several years and several Synods. Matters such as this are covered by special Bills which require a two-thirds majority of the clergy and a two-thirds majority of the laity, voting separately. The House of Bishops also, of course, may vote as a separate House, although this does not occur very often. However, it did occur on the occasion of the debate on the ordination of women priests.

Interestingly, although the members of the House of Representatives must vote in public, by walking through lobbies, the House of Bishops votes in private, so that any divisions are not to be seen by the ordinary members of the Church. Whether this is a good or a bad thing, I am not sure; Ireland is a small place and the Church of Ireland is a small Church. People become aware, or think they become aware, through rumour or other means, that there are differing opinions among the various bishops and it might be better to have an open vote rather than to have rumours of this sort circulating. An interesting comparison might be made with the situation which has arisen in the Roman Catholic Church where the Bishop of Ferns has sought an open debate on the issue of married clergy, and where there appears to be distinct disagreement among the various members of the Hierarchy on both the issue itself, and on the right of the Bishop of Ferns to raise it in public.

On the whole, however, I feel that the issue of the ordination of women was handled extremely well in the General Synod under the guidance of the Primate as President. As a result, I hope that those who opposed the move did not feel as alienated as seems to have happened in other Churches, and certainly there does not appear to have been the sort of overt division which has unfortunately occurred in the Church of England.

Room for improvement?

It can been seen that the structures of the Church of Ireland are inclusive and democratic in nature, although, of course, to describe a Church as a democracy would be misleading. As is the case in most large bodies, there is a considerable element of 'management' in the democratic function of the General Synod and the diocesan synods, and it is fairly rare to find a bitterly fought election for any particular office. However, while there is a great deal of respect for the authority of the bishops, there is also quite a healthy ability in the General Synod to challenge their views and I have seen at least one occasion where the House of Representatives in the Synod clearly voted down an effort by the House of Bishops to direct the result of a certain debate. By and large the balance of power operates pretty effectively.

There are, however, other criticisms which can be made of the General Synod in particular. Some of these were validly and cogently set out by J. L. B. Deane,* in a paper presented to the Standing Committee, just before his retirement from the Office of Honorary Secretary of the General Synod in 1994. He argued that the General Synod was far too large and should be reduced to a number of 300, with 100 clerical and 200 lay members.

At present, the membership is limited by the fact that no expenses are paid to members and that membership requires the commitment of attending for three days in the middle of the working week. This makes it extremely difficult for anyone in full-time employment, who is not sufficiently senior to be able to take three days off, or who is unwilling to sacrifice three days of their annual holiday period to be a functioning member of the General Synod. Mr Deane points out in his paper that the lay

---

*In compiling this paper I am indebted to Mr Deane's indispensible *Church of Ireland Handbook* (APCK, Dublin).

membership of the Church, as far as income is concerned, varies from millionaires to deserted wives 'who may or may not be receiving the maintenance to which they are entitled'. Membership of the General Synod can impose considerable financial hardship on those who are not well off and, indeed, such persons probably avoid being elected to the body. This skews the membership in a certain direction – middle-aged and middle-class, perhaps?

One of the difficulties of the General Synod meeting is that timetable pressure can result in important reports receiving very slight consideration. If the ordinary Church membership is to be kept involved in the work which is being done by the committees of the General Synod, this situation needs to be changed or reorganised in some way. However, it has proved extremely difficult to persuade the General Synod that any such reforms are necessary. Mr Deane firmly points out that 'from time to time there are references to the General Synod as being an exercise in communication, or a place where one meets old friends and makes new ones, or an occasion which is accompanied by a social function. I do not undervalue these but they are peripheral. The primary functions of the General Synod are legislative and administrative. It meets to discharge the business which is laid before it.'

In proposing his ideas for reform, which in my view are rational and at least deserve to be properly discussed, he does not really expect that they will be accepted. I fear that he may be right but, perhaps in a triumph of optimism over realism, I think that some version of reform of the General Synod is probably necessary to make it into a more effective and efficient body.

However, that is not to underestimate its qualities and indeed the qualities of all the Church structures which I have here outlined. In summary, it might be said that while a very considerable amount of power is given to the laity, a very great deal of commitment is demanded of them in giving the time and energy to ensure that all these structures function properly. In some of the more sparsely populated dioceses in the West and South, almost too much, I think, is demanded of the relatively few

Church members by way of service to committees and other structures. It is, however, a commitment which they most faithfully give, year in and year out. Perhaps the small numbers may also have one or two good side-effects, as I noticed, for instance, that the only diocese in Ireland that has 100% female representation in its lay membership of the Standing Committee of the General Synod is the diocese of Tuam.

If I might put it this way, I think that most members of the Church of Ireland feel reasonably comfortable with the way in which authority in the Church is distributed. As in all institutions with human members, there are the customary number of grumbles, complaints, queries and whinges, but these are usually of a fairly minor nature, and I believe that in particular the lay members of the Church value the important part which they play in its structure, organisation and major decisions.

Authority in the Methodist Church

Gillian Kingston

As it was in the beginning ...

'Nothing can be more simple, nothing more rational, than the
Methodist discipline: it is entirely founded on common sense,
particularly applying the general rules of scripture. Anyone determined to save his soul may be united with them. But this desire must be evidenced by three marks: Avoiding all known sin;
doing good after his power; and attending all the ordinances of
God.' So declared John Wesley, inadvertent founder of Methodism,
in a sermon dated October 17th, 1787.[1]

Though the word 'authority' is not used, this passage neatly
summarises what John Wesley understood by the term: it is
scriptural, that is to say, God-given; it is reasonable; and it is life-
changing. The Wesleyan emphasis is on discipline rather than
authority, though obviously the notions are related.

> 204. Discipline in the Church is an exercise of that spiritual
> authority which the Lord Jesus has appointed in his Church.
> The ends contemplated by discipline are the maintenance of
> the purity of the Church, the spiritual benefit of its members,
> and the honour of our Lord.[2]

John Wesley never intended to separate from the Church of
England and form a new Church. Rather he sought to establish a
network, a 'connexion', to use his own term, of fellowship
groups within that Church for the mutual support and enrichment of committed Christians. Authority within the Christian
community, as he saw it, was the prerogative of the established
Church, and he had no intention of departing from that.
Preaching in Cork in 1789, he says:

> I hold all the doctrines of the Church of England. I love her

liturgy. I approve her plan of discipline, and only wish it could be put into execution. I do not knowingly vary from any rule of the Church, unless in those few instances where I judge, and as far as I judge, there is an absolute necessity.[3]

But even groups within a Church need discipline and, in 1743, John and Charles Wesley (the latter the great hymn writer) put their names to a document entitled 'The Nature, Design and General Rules of the United Societies in London, Bristol, Kingswood, Newcastle-upon-Tyne, etc'.[4] These indicate that:

- the society is to be divided into 'classes', each with its leader, who is responsible for the spiritual well-being of the members, meeting with each one every week and with the appointed minister of the society;

- all that is required for membership is 'a desire to flee from the wrath to come, to be saved from … sin,' and that this should be seen by the avoiding of evil in lifestyle;

- further, those who desire salvation should show that desire by actively doing good in their community;

- thirdly, they should be diligent in attendance at worship and the Lord's Supper, in reading the scriptures, in prayer and in fasting;

- those who habitually break the rules are to be admonished, tolerated for a time, then disallowed membership.

That such discipline became necessary is evident from a variety of entries in Wesley's *Journal*:

Friday, August 17th 1750: I preached in Ludgvan at noon and at Newlyn in the evening. Through all Cornwall I find the societies have suffered great loss from want of discipline. Wisely said the ancients, 'The soul and body make a man; the Spirit and discipline make a Christian.'[5]

April 1st 1758 (in Dublin): All the evenings of the following week we had numerous congregations. Nothing is wanting here but rigorous discipline, which is more needful here than in any other nation ….[6]

A system of quarterly membership tickets identified those who were faithful members of the societies from those whose attendance left somewhat to be desired. 'By these it was easily distinguished, when the society was to meet apart, who were members of it or not. These also supplied us with a quiet and inoffensive method of removing any disorderly member.'[7]

A further refinement of the class system led to the setting up of bands, groups of exclusively men or women, who met for deeper fellowship and sharing. Then in 1744, some five years after the first societies were formed, John Wesley called his first conference of preachers in London, with a view to giving him 'their advice concerning the best method of carrying on the work of God'.[8] So, in the early days of the Methodist movement, were born the structures for discipline and rule within the societies.

... is now ...

l. Authority within the Church

The Conference is the supreme court of the Church and the final authority within the Church in all matters of both doctrine and discipline; as such, it regulates decisions made in the other courts of the Church,

> All members and ministers of the Church are subject to its government and discipline, and are under the jurisdiction and care of the appropriate Courts of the Church in all matters of doctrine, worship, discipline and order in accordance with rules and regulations from time to time made by the Conference.[9]

Both members and ministers are people under discipline, and continued membership in the Methodist Church depends on their fulfiling the duties and responsibilities of that membership.

> Continuance in Church membership shall depend on general spiritual fitness, which shall be manifested by Christian conduct, attendance at public worship, at the Sacrament of the Lord's Supper, at meetings for Christian fellowship, and at

the other means of grace so far as can be reasonably expected. If a member persistently fails to fulfil these conditions, he shall be regarded as having severed his connection with the Church and his name shall be removed from the membership roll.[10]

A minister of the church is a member who has been 'separated' for ordained ministry *within* the ministry of the whole church.

> ... a minister is constituted by the Call of God, the consent of the members of the Church, the election of the Conference and the ordination to the office and work of a minister in the Church of God by prayer and the laying on of hands.[11]

38. The office of a minister is to win and watch over souls as he that must give account. He must not only feed and guide the flock by regular and faithful preaching, teaching and pastoral visitation, but also recognise that his effectiveness under God in all things will depend on the quality of his life and witness, and his ability so to discipline himself that he give no offence or occasion to stumble to any. Further, he must act with particular responsibility in matters where his practice or use may be the cause of physical or moral harm to some.[12]

So says the *Manual of Laws of the Methodist Church in Ireland*. First compiled in 1814, the Manual has undergone a number of revisions, the most recent being in 1976. Complemented each year by directives from the Conference, it is the indispensable guide to discipline and rule within the Methodist Church, both for members and for ministers.

The 'Courts of the Church', to which reference has been made, are based on the historic groupings established by Wesley:

- the *Leaders' Meeting*, charged with the administration of the local Society (congregation) and its constituent classes. It consists of the minister(s), the class leaders, the local preachers, elected representatives of the congregation and other local officers.

- the *Quarterly Meeting*, which administers the affairs of a Circuit, being a group of one or more societies, in the charge of a Superintendent minister. It is attended by the minister(s), members of all the Leaders' Meetings and other local officers and representatives.

- the *District Synod*, which administers the common affairs of a group of circuits within a district. Directed by a minister elected as chairman, the Synod has a ministerial session attended by all ministers and probationers, and a representative session, attended by ministers and lay people.

- the *Conference*, the governing body of the Church, is attended by ministers and lay people in equal numbers. There is a ministerial session, which deals with the discipline, admission and expulsion of ministers, and a representative session for all other matters.

- Based on the divine revelation recorded in Holy Scripture, the doctrines of the evangelical faith held by Methodism find expression in Wesley's *Notes on the New Testament* and the first four volumes of his sermons. These are intended to set a standard of preaching and belief rather than to impose a system of theology. The Conference is the final authority within the Church on all matters concerning interpretation of its doctrine.

The first Methodist Conference in Ireland was held in Limerick in 1752. It was chaired by John Wesley himself. With a few exceptions, the Irish Conference has always been chaired by the successor of John Wesley, the President of the Methodist Church in Britain, who is thus also President of the Irish Conference, though not of the Methodist Church in Ireland. The Methodist Church in Ireland elects the Vice-President of the Conference who is, by virtue of this office, President of the Church.

2. Wider answerability

The Conference of the Methodist Church in Ireland is the supreme authority *in* the church. However, the Methodist Church in Ireland belongs to a number of bodies within both the world Methodist community and the ecumenical community, and thus is subscribes, within appropriate terms, to those bodies.

The changes within Europe over the last decade, involving the development of the European Community and the breakup of the Communist bloc, have challenged the Churches to rethink their role in society. The Methodist Churches in Europe perceived a need for a forum for co-operation and exchange of information. This led to the founding of the *European Methodist Council* which includes almost all European Methodist Churches.

The Council has a number of standing committees on issues such as theological studies and mission, and it relates to several already existing bodies, including the *European Methodist Youth Council* and the European branches of the *World Federation of Methodist Women*. Its role, however, is consultative only, and its decisions are *not* binding on the member churches.

The role of the *World Methodist Council* is similar on a world level: it does not legislate for the member Churches, of which there are over sixty, nor does it seek to invade their autonomy. It does seek, however, to serve in the widest sense, and to give unity to the common witness of the member Churches. Meeting every five years, it receives reports from its commissions and committees. Importantly, these include those of the International Commissions in dialogue with other world communions. The reports are received and passed down to the individual member Churches. The process of reception and implementation is the concern of the Churches rather than of the Council.

The Methodist Church in Ireland belongs to a number of ecumenical bodies at various levels: the *Irish Council of Churches* and the *Irish Inter-Church Meeting* at the national level; the *Council of Churches of Britain and Ireland* within these islands; the *Council of European Churches* at European level and, at world level, the *World Council of Churches*.

...And ever shall be ?

As we have seen, the structures and and usages of the Methodist Church have their origins in its beginnings as a movement *within* the Church of England rather than as a deliberate split-off. Had the Church of the time felt less threatened by Wesley's evangelical methods, his original vision might have prevailed.

AUTHORITY IN THE METHODIST CHURCH   85

However, many of those who flocked to hear him were the unchurched from the working class of the time, those to whom and for whom the established Church made no appeal, and who would not, in any case, have felt welcome within its portals. These people saw no good reason why they should be obedient to the authority of a Church to which they had never belonged.

Thus, early in the story of Methodism there was a tension between belonging and not belonging, between an adherence to the discipline of the Anglican Church as advocated and observed by John Wesley himself, who was very much an authoritarian figure, and a Methodist *sensus fidelium*, whereby the members of the movement had a say in its organisation.

History and theory, however admirable, are no substitute for praxis, and the question needs to be asked as to how the Methodist system of authority/discipline works in other times and other places; has this tension been resolved?

There is in Methodism a sense of the fundamental equality of all members, lay and ordained, women and men: all are people under discipline, all are responsible for and to each other. The differences are differences of function rather than differences in kind. The structures of the Church allow for lay participation at all levels of the Church's governance, and one person's vote in any matter is as good as another's, lay or ordained.

Any system which works on democratic principles is of necessity more fluid and flexible than one which works by dictat. Much may depend on those who, in any given year, are elected to represent their circuits at Conference. There can be a tendency for lobbying groups to attempt to swing voting their direction on any given issue.

At a time when authority is being questioned in all areas of human community, when it might appear that 'do your own thing' appears to be the order of the day, the Methodist Church is no more immune to challenges to its discipline than any other. It may be that a system of discipline for a movement, evolved in a time when the majority of members were illiterate and unread, cannot well serve a recognised Church in a time of almost universal education. It may be that, in common with other Churches in a time of falling Church membership, the Church may be loath to appear authoritarian for fear of alienating would-be members, so challenges to its discipline may go unchecked.

The old tension between established order and freedom of spirit still exists in Methodism: what is important is that that tension is allowed to be fruitful and creative rather than divisive and destructive. To repeat a saying often used by John Wesley, 'The soul and the body make a man; the Spirit and discipline make a Christian.' What is true of the individual is equally true of any community of individuals naming the name of Christ and claiming to be 'the people called Methodist.'

Notes

1. Wesley, John, Sermon CVII, 'In God's Vineyard', *Works*, vol 7, pp 202-213. John Mason, 14, City Road, London, 1830.

2. *Manual of Laws*, Methodist Church in Ireland, 1976. # 204

3. Wesley, John, Sermon, 'The Ministerial Office' *Works*, vol 7, pp 273-281.

4. 'The Nature, Design and General Rules of the United Societies in London, Bristol, Kingswood and Newcastle-upon-Tyne', etc. *Works*, vol 8, pp 269-271. Also in the *Manual of Laws*, #3 pp 32-36.

5. Wesley, John, *Journal*, vol III, p 491. Edited by Nehemiah Curnock 1909. Charles H. Kelly, 25-35 City Road, London.

6. *Journal*, vol IV, p 258.

7. Wesley, John, 'A Plain Account of the People called Methodists', *Works*, vol 8, pp 248-268.

8. Wesley, John, Minutes of Several Conversations between Rev John Wesley and others, *Works,* vol 8, pp 299-338.

9. *Manual of Laws* , section V, p 18.

10. *Manual of Laws,* # 13, p 39.

11. *Manual of Laws,* section IV, p 18.

12. *Manual of Laws,* # 3, 8, p 46.

Authority in the Presbyterian Church

Terence McCaughey

It if difficult to generalise about the exercise of authority within that large family of Churches in Europe, North America and indeed throughout the world, which are called 'Reformed' or 'Presbyterian'. Since most of them have their point of origin in the sixteenth-century Reformation led by John Calvin and his associates, one could do worse than look briefly at what Calvin himself had to say on the matter. One thing is certain, that in all those Churches like the Church of England which retained an episcopal rather than presbyterian form of government, but nevertheless were largely Calvinist in their theology throughout the sixteenth and seventeenth centuries, the centre of all authority lay in the word of God as it is to be heard in the scriptures of the Old and New Testaments.

For Calvin, as for Luther and Bucer before him, it was the word of God which constituted the Church and, under the guidance of the Spirit, was understood to sustain it. He followed his predecessors in admitting only two criteria, both of them, as he believed, verifiable and objective. 'Wherever we see the word of God purely preached, and the sacraments administered according to the institution of Christ, we must not doubt that there is a Church.'

So he comprehended under 'Church' all those in the world who 'make the same profession of honouring God in Jesus Christ, have the same baptism as evidence of their faith, and who, by partaking of the Supper, claim to have unity in doctrine and charity, who accept the word of God and seek to protect the preaching of it in obedience to the commandment of Jesus Christ.' Calvin goes on in the same passage to allow for the imperfections and hypocrisy which may infect the membership. Nevertheless, he says, 'We are commanded to hold the visible Church in honour and keep ourselves in communion with it.'

Calvin recognised, of course, that the 'invisible Church is known only to God' and, furthermore, that God was entirely free to communicate the divine grace otherwise than by the pastors' preaching and the use of the sacraments. But whereas God is free in this regard that does not mean that we who are called are similarly free. For, by the very fact that God has called the Church into being, we are bound to her and to the means of grace entrusted to her, as we must inevitably be gratefully bound to any gift of God, simply because it *is* God's.

Calvin did not see ecclesiastical discipline as one of the *essential* characters of the Church, but he did acknowledge it to be unavoidable if good order was to be maintained. But his prevailing model for the exercise of discipline within the Church was educational rather than judicial, and he appears to have believed that offenders should be brought to repentance before all else. The question as to how to bring them to that remained open, as often as not. John Knox, when he visited Geneva, described it as 'a parfyte schule of Christ' and so, at its best, it may have been. But sixteenth-century schools were often harsh!

Even in the rising city-states of Europe, where the burghers could stand up for themselves, there was a tendency for the Churches of the Calvinist reform to hanker after theocracy. In Scotland, where the bourgeoisie was small and less developed, that tendency proved even stronger – especially given the peculiar line of Scottish history. Scottish Calvinism is, of course, particularly significant for us in Ireland, and deserves a moment's consideration.

Very shortly after the Protestant Reformation was officially declared by the Scottish Estates (i.e. parliament) to have happened in 1560, it became clear that the Reformed Church in Scotland was going to be difficult. The Queen, Mary Stuart, widow of the Dauphin of France, had no notion of becoming a Protestant, and confessional difference between her and her subjects led to her ecclesiastical functions as prince simply falling into the hands of the Church leaders.

Forty-three years later her son, King James VI, became James I of England as well, and left Edinburgh for London. And a century further on, Scotland lost its independent parliament. By the Act of Union a Scottish oligarchy retained control of the legal system, education, poor relief and the Church of Scotland. Those who controlled these institutions could do so without fear of interference from London. There can be no doubt that, as the eighteenth century wore on, the distinction between Church and State blurred increasingly and, at local level, the parish minister and his elders more and more assumed the role of local government. This is the state of affairs which Robert Burns and others protested against and satirised.

The Scottish Presbyterians who came to the north of Ireland could not hope to control the society in which they now found themselves. They turned inwards and ran a society within a society, laying a good deal of emphasis on doctrinal correctness and internal discipline. They did not enjoy the civil rights of the members of the established Church; they could operate schools only with permission from the Church of Ireland bishop; their marriages were not recognised; they could not vote for or sit in the parliament in College Green, and they paid tithes to a Church they did not attend.

Inside their own Church they exercised a fairly strict discipline and, as is the case of the majority Church in Ireland, this discipline was closely associated with participation in the sacrament of the Lord's Supper. So strict did the discipline surrounding admission to the sacrament become that, especially after the great evangelical revivals of the eighteenth and nineteenth centuries, a majority of parishioners feared to take communion at all for fear of 'eating and drinking damnation to themselves.' Clearly the minister and elders, who examined persons coming forward, exercised enormous and even frightening authority. Today all that has changed, or is changing.

The structures now

The member Churches of the World Alliance of Reformed Churches, which includes almost all of those who call themselves 'Reformed' or 'Presbyterian', do not all organise themselves in quite the same way. For instance, the largest member-Church outside of the United States is the Reformed Church of Hungary which has bishops as well as presbyteries. John Knox, the Scottish reformer, divided the newly reformed Church of Scotland into four or five regions, each overseen by an executive officer known as a Superintendant.

One thing, however, is common to all these Churches: that is, an emphasis on *collective* rather than individual *episcopé* or oversight. So *presbyteries*, the parishes within an area originally corresponding to the diocesan boundaries, are overseen by all the ministers of that area, each one 'marked' by an *elder* from the various congregations. The Moderator is simply the annually elected chairperson of presbytery, and has no executive or pastoral function within it.

Presbyteries oversee the work within their bounds collectively. Individual ministers are responsible finally, not to the congregation which 'called' them to minister in that parish, but rather to the presbytery which either ordained them or installed them in that particular charge. Elders are officers of a particular parish and, though elected by the people, are usually ordained by the parish minister to oversee the parish with him. They cannot meet in his absence.

Once a year all ministers in the Church, together with representative elders to a number equal to the number of ministers, meet in General Assembly. The Assembly receives reports and suggested resolutions from its boards and committees. The decision as to what reports to 'receive' and what resolutions to pass lies with the Assembly itself and its decision is binding on all presbyteries and parishes.

This all looks very democratic, and often commands admiration from outside observers. There are factors, however, that impede its effective operation:

(1) The elders tend to be either self-employed or retired, middle-class, middle-aged, and male. The decisions of Assembly will, especially when it comes to crunch issues on which elders vote but tend not to speak, reflect the prejudices to be associated with the middle-class, middle-aged male.

(2) A question, which is perhaps more philosophical than practical, also arises. Is 'winning a debate' and the subsequent vote the most appropriate way for a Christian community to arrive at decisions?

(3) Finally, there is a question about the authority of the decisions reached – a question it is appropriate to finish with, since it applies to all our Churches.

There is a clear obligation on me, as a member of the Presbyterian Church in Ireland, to abide by the Assembly's decision on, say, ministerial pensions. But what about resolutions put to the Assembly on nuclear testing, the Downing Street Declaration, or sanctions against Indonesia? On these questions it may be possible for two groups of equally sincere Christians to disagree.

I am glad if 'my side' wins the vote. But if they 'lose', I will probably still work as before for CND or the East Timor Committee or whatever. That is fine, perhaps. But where does it leave the alleged 'authority' of the General Assembly?

Both Calvinist and Catholic experience suggests that authority is ever exercised only temporarily and provisionally. Like faith itself, it is not the property of those who exercise it, but rather a gift to be handled with care.

Afterword

Seán Mac Réamoinn

It is clear that the issue of authority is fundamental to many, if not all, the other issues which preoccupy Christians today. We have seen how its misuse, or flaws in its exercise and its structures, may do severe damage to the fabric of the Church, betray and alienate her members, and impair her witness and mission.

But it is also clear that authority, seen as a gift and exercised as service, can bring a positive enrichment to the pilgrim Church in her journey towards truth. For it can cast light on the problems and challenges of Christian life in society – poverty and property, sexuality and marriage, education, technological development and the 'information revolution' – as well as those questions more specifically of Church concern: language and worship, clericalism, the ministry of women.

We hope to address some of these issues, and perhaps others, in future explorations.

The Contributors

BILL COSGRAVE is parish priest of Monageer in the diocese of Ferns. Formerly, he was lecturer in moral theology at St Peter's College, Wexford.

LOUIS McREDMOND, lawyer, historian, journalist and broadcaster, was a newspaper reporter at Vatican II and Dublin correspondent of *The Tablet* from 1966 to 1995.

MARY McALEESE is a Professor and Pro Vice Chancellor of The Queen's University, Belfast. She was a member of the episcopal delegation of the Roman Catholic Church to the New Ireland Forum in 1984.

CATHERINE McGUINNESS is a Judge of the Circuit Court and Chairperson of the Forum for Peace and Reconciliation. She is a member of the General Synod of the Church of Ireland.

GILLIAN KINGSTON is a Methodist local preacher, a member of the Methodist-Roman Catholic International Commission, a President of the Council of Churches of Britain and Ireland, and a member of the Board of The Irish School of Ecumenics.

TERENCE McCAUGHEY, who is a Minister of the Presbyterian Church in Ireland, is a Senior Lecturer in the Irish Department, Trinity College, Dublin, and also teaches in the School of Biblical and Theological Studies.

SEÁN MAC RÉAMOINN, broadcaster and writer, is a prominent commentator on religious and cultural affairs.

COLUMBA EXPLORATIONS

Columba Explorations is to be an occasional series of slim volumes exploring current issues as they arise in the Church and society.

If you would like to be informed of future volumes, please complete the form below.

Please send me information on future *Columba Explorations:*

Name:_____

Address:_____

_____

_____

Please return to:
the columba bookservice
93 The Rise, Mount Merrion, Blackrock,
Co Dublin, Ireland
Telephone: (01) 2832954 Fax: (01)2883770
Orders: (01)2836236
E-mail: columba@internet-eireann.ie